GREAT WESTEI
BRANCH LINE MODELLING

PART TWO
PROTOTYPE BUILDINGS, FITTINGS
& TRAFFIC OPERATION

by Stephen Williams

FOR HELEN

Previous page: *Diesel railcar No. 30 at Raglan, working the 7.46 ex Pontypool Road–Monmouth service on 24th March 1951.* **This page:** *Faringdon station c.1920.*
W. A. CAMWELL and L & GRP, CTY. DAVID & CHARLES

ACKNOWLEDGEMENTS

Once again I am happy to acknowledge the assistance provided by a number of individuals in the preparation of this, the second volume, in the study of Great Western branch lines. In particular, I am indebted to John Copsey who kindly spent some of his own research time in copying records of traffic operation which he had located at the Public Records Office at Kew. He also made available records of coach workings from his private collection and for this I am most grateful.

I am also indebted to Austin Attewell for the use of so many of his fine photographs. The incidental detail of the railway which Austin has recorded is critical to the creation of good models and the book is much the better for his contribution. I also acknowledge, with thanks, the use of photographs from the Welsh Industrial & Maritime Museum, the Historical Model Railway Society, Lens of Sutton, Paul Karau, Roger Carpenter, Pat Garland, David & Charles for the use of L & GRP photos, and W. R. Burton (Brunel University: Mowat collection).

Finally, sincere thanks to Paul and June at Wild Swan for their skilled and sympathetic work in producing this book.

Designed by Paul Karau
Printed by Amadeus Press, Cleckheaton, W. Yorkshire

Published by
WILD SWAN PUBLICATIONS LTD.
1–3 Hagbourne Road, Didcot, Oxon OX11 8DP

INTRODUCTION

Part 2 of the study of Great Western branch line modelling continues and concludes the examination of the prototype. The central tenet of this work is that accurate and convincing models of Great Western branch lines can only be based upon a sound understanding of the characteristics of the real thing. To that end, Parts 1 and 2 have sought to examine systematically and in detail, the nature of real branch lines, as a preface to Part 3 which will examine their translation into model form. The previous volume was primarily concerned with the physical layout of branch stations, the construction of the permanent way and signalling. In Part 2 I propose to extend the discussion to a consideration of buildings and their associated fittings, and conclude with an outline essay on the nature of branch line traffic operation.

Readers who are already familiar with Part 1 will know that part of the purpose of these books is to illustrate the enormous variety that was to be encountered amongst the branches of the Great Western. The uninitiated perhaps adopt, too readily, a stereotypical view of these lines. But, as I hope the chapters which follow will reinforce, real branches showed infinite variation. As a devotee of the Great Western, I am perhaps a shade biased, but I am convinced that there is inspiration for a lifetime's modelling amongst these fascinating lines, provided we are prepared to look.

Stephen Williams

CHAPTER ONE

BUILDINGS

IN my opening chapter in Part 1, I tried to argue that rather than being marked by a predictable uniformity, Great Western branch lines were actually very varied. That variety is not so apparent within the trackwork and signalling systems which we considered in the final two chapters in Part 1, but becomes much more prominent when buildings and their related fixtures and fittings are reviewed.

For modellers, buildings are especially important elements within a project. Scratch-built structures, in particular, will absorb a significant proportion of the time expended upon the construction of the layout but they will help to create the character and atmosphere that we are seeking in our model. I suspect, too, that many of us choose particular prototypes for models partly on the basis of the visual appeal of the buildings and it would be very rare to find such consideration playing no part in the choice of subject.

The character of buildings and their fittings also helps to create an identifiable scene. When our model is of an imaginary setting, one of the principal ways in which we can indicate the company ownership is through the style of building, the design of nameboards, platform seats, lamps etc.,

and the colours in which they are painted. Get these right and you take a large step towards an authentic model.

The next two chapters attempt to provide a summary of styles of building deployed on Great Western branch lines, together with the equipment to be found in and around the stations. Chapter 1 will focus upon the 'major structures': station buildings, goods sheds, signal boxes and engine sheds. Chapter 2 examines minor structures (footbridges, cattle docks, lamp sheds, lock-ups and the like); 'fixtures and fittings' (items such as seats, lamps, nameboards and fencing), and concludes with a résumé of styles of painting. Much fuller detail on this latter aspect can be obtained in the Historical Model Railway Society's *Great Western Way*. This is a valuable source but don't take every word as gospel as there are errors and instances where subsequent research has thrown additional and sometimes contradictory light upon the subject. Other useful sources include Adrian Vaughan's *Pictorial Record of Great Western Architecture* (OPC), a fascinating book although most of the text and illustrations deal with main line scenes rather than branches. I also like Chris Leigh's two books *GWR Country Stations* (Ian Allan)

which provide much more in the way of branch line illustrations. (The bibliography gives details on these publications and other relevant sources.)

STATION BUILDINGS

Let us start our review with what most of us would consider as the main building in the scene, the station itself. It is helpful, I think, to draw a distinction between buildings constructed by the GWR or a contractor working to the company's instructions and those built by independent companies. We should re-emphasise, too, that the independently constructed station was likely to be in the majority. The GWR sometimes replaced buildings which it inherited with one of its familiar standard designs, but if the original building was satisfactory, it would tend to continue in service. This diversity of origin was one of the principal sources of variety in branch stations.

The earliest stations built by the GWR were designed by Brunel and he established styles of building which were followed for several decades, persisting after the great man had died in 1859. His widespread involvement in railway construction also ensured that his designs were

Ilminster, designed by Brunel for the Bristol and Exeter Railway in his 'Italianate' style.　　　LENS OF SUTTON

The train shed was a common feature on mid-19th century stations and many, like this fine example at Cheddar, survived into BR days. This picture features 2–6–2T No. 5527 on a Strawberry Special for Yatton on 23rd June 1953.   P. J. GARLAND

Chard, perhaps the most elaborate of the Italianate stations. Note how the style of the main building has here been extended to the train shed.   L & GRP CTY. DAVID & CHARLES

2–4–0 'Metro' tank engine No. 5 at Chard with a local train for Taunton. The leading vehicle is one of the early pattern six-wheel 'Siphons' with a single arc roof.

H. C. CASSERLEY

A simpler style of overall roof at Tavistock. LENS OF SUTTON

used on lines which at that stage were independent or only loosely associated with the GWR, but which subsequently became a part of the Great Western. Thus his influence spread all the way to Penzance via the South Devon, Cornwall and West Cornwall Railways; into South Wales on the South Wales and Taff Vale Railways; to the Midlands along the Oxford, Worcester and Wolverhampton Railway, and towards the south coast with the Berks & Hants and Wiltshire, Somerset and Weymouth Railways. He also worked on lines which did not become a part of the GWR, for example the Bristol and Gloucester line which was taken over by the Midland Railway but which had several excellent examples of Brunel's designs.

It is probably more realistic to talk of Brunel *style* buildings since it is very apparent that having set a style, Brunel was content to leave his assistants to prepare designs to his guidelines. These were often competent and experienced engineers, and several, J. H. Bertram, R. P. Brereton and W. Lancaster Owen, to name but three,

rose to positions of importance. So many of the stations which look like Brunel's work were actually the designs of others.

Studies of the Brunel style of building for the GWR suggest that three main types can be recognised, although each was subject to considerable variation in details of design. The first type was a 'Gothic' style, reminiscent of Perpendicular architecture of the Tudor period. A large number of small, wayside stations were designed by Brunel in this style, the best surviving example being at Culham. This was not a design, however, that was typical of branch stations, and in the photo surveys which I have conducted as background research, I have not identified an instance of these designs on a branch.

Alongside his Gothic design, Brunel produced stations in an 'Italianate' style, small chalet stations with distinctive round arched windows and doors and broad hipped roofs extending to provide roadside and trackside canopies. These were usually built in brick and stone (although a restored timber example survives at

Charlbury on the Worcester line) and were widely scattered. Examples occurred at Ivybridge (South Devon), Bridgend (South Wales), Yatton (Somerset), Mortimer and Theale (Berkshire). These were all main line stations, but examples did occur on branches, one of the best instances being the Taunton to Chard line, originally built for the Bristol and Exeter Railway. Chard was a more elaborate development of the simpler design though smaller stations on the line, notably Hatch, were very like the other examples given.

The third type of station with which Brunel was associated incorporated the famous trainshed or overall roof. This is an excellent example of the perpetuation of a Brunel design by others. The overall roof first appeared on larger main line stations between Paddington and Bristol but designs were copied and adapted at many other locations on primary and secondary routes. Some of the most popular branch stations with modellers possessed these roofs, Ashburton, Moretonhampstead and Thame being prominent instances. Larger branch stations with overall roofs included Tavistock, Henley-on-Thames, Merthyr Tydfil and Falmouth.

None of these branch stations was actually the work of Brunel although their design shows his influence most strongly. Gradually, though, the pattern of building began to change, although some branch line stations showed a clear line of descent from Brunel's work. The lovely building at Marlow, erected in 1873, gives an example where the 'Italianate' style was still very influential, especially in the design of the doors and windows. However, the typical pattern for smaller stations in the 1880s was much more prosaic and we see signs of the emergence of the standardised styles of building for which the GWR became renowned. Construction of these later Victorian stations was commonly in brick with very distinctive fenestration – rectangular and elongated – rectangular windows being placed in twos and threes, set beneath a curved lintel with a brick arch above. Chimney stacks, in contrast to Brunel's magnificent creations, were usually fairly plain. Nice examples of this type of station on branch or secondary routes were to be found at Stourbridge Town, Ross on Wye and Winchester and, as a main line example, Kingham. The stations at Stourbridge, Ross and Winchester were ornamented with the addition of sloping roof

Winchester, built to a design which was popular in the 1880s and was repeated at a number of secondary and main line stations. COLLECTION D. LITTLEFAIR

'turrets', bedecked with wrought iron-work. These particular designs are usually attributed to J. E. Danks, who was also responsible for some interesting main line stations, most notably perhaps, Slough.

At about the same time (I cannot pin-point the precise date), the GWR introduced a most distinctive pattern of wooden station building. They were

unusual insofar as the main framework for the structure was on the outside with panel infills of vertical planking. I must admit that I rather like these buildings and they make nice models. More to the point, several examples appeared on branch lines during the latter part of the 19th century. The unusual structure in this style at Yelverton is well known but the same method

Less prestigious locations were favoured with simpler, but rather attractive wooden structures. These had a distinctive pattern of external framing and often, as in this example from Brynamman in South Wales, the roof was extended to provide the platform awning.

NATIONAL RAILWAY MUSEUM

Culkerton provides an excellent example of these late 19th century wooden stations. A very similar design from Toller is now under restoration on the Dart Valley line near Totnes.
COURTESY LIONEL PADIN

The strange, polygonal building at Yelverton was also executed in the same style.
ROYE ENGLAND

Newcastle Emlyn and Calne both exemplify the first of the new designs for standard stations introduced at the turn of the century. Note the characteristic roof light on the building at Newcastle Emlyn. The two buildings also illustrate the GWR standard 'flat' platform canopy.

G. M. PERKINS and LENS OF SUTTON

of construction was used at Culkerton and the original building at Tetbury, Toller Percorum in Dorset, Fowey, Shipston-on-Stour and the down side building at Winchester. Dartmouth, the GWR's famous station without a railway, was built in a similar style but with a more ornate roof featuring wrought ironwork.

The standard designs which are most readily recognised, however, were produced around the turn of the century, although there is some evidence to suggest that these may have been derived from a slightly earlier design of the type which appeared at, for example, Shiplake. There were two basic patterns, both stoutly constructed in red brick with bull-nosed engineering 'blues' often used for plinths, corners and sometimes, door and window reveals. Roofs were slated. The first type was provided with a hipped roof, typically with a triangular skylight at one end which helped illuminate the gentlemen's toilet. The canopy used with this design was normally a pitched roof which was bracketed to the main building. The second type was actually a flat roof design but the canopy, again with a pitched roof, extended right across the building, such that the flat roof to the building was not immediately apparent.

Introduction of these designs coincided with a period of significant expansion in

Two further examples of the new standard stations, although here with the more usual style of awning. Yealmpton was a comparatively rare example of a stone-built station of this design. St. Agnes was extensively modified during a phase of track development (see Part 1, p. 96).
LENS OF SUTTON

the company's system; the South Wales Direct line via Badminton, the Birmingham Direct line through Bicester and the new route from Birmingham to Bristol through Stratford and Winchcombe being the major projects. Dozens of new standard stations were built on these main line routes but examples also found their way onto branches. By this stage of the railway's history, there were

few branches still under construction, but renewal of older structures at this time usually saw one of these buildings utilised.

Examples of the first style were located at Wargrave, Calne, Fawley and Newcastle Emlyn, with some rare stone-built examples of the same design on the Yealmpton branch at Brixton Road, Billacombe and Yealmpton itself. The flat-roofed style with its overall canopy was

G. W. R. Station, Lambourn.

stone moulding, were raised slightly above the line of the roof to provide a raised parapet. On the roof line were positioned the ornate chimney stacks, almost always three in number, each sporting a pair or trio of vertical stone deflectors. The whole ensemble was beautifully compact and neatly proportioned. Adjoining one end of the building there was normally a flat-roofed structure, built in a matching style, which housed the toilets and various stores. The platform canopy was bracketed to the main wall and possessed a deep, saw-tooth valance which differed quite noticeably from standard GWR designs. These Clarke buildings make lovely subjects for models and readers who would like to know more about them are encouraged to consult Gerry Beale's article in *British Railway Journal* No. 8 or Brian

Lambourn with the alternative style of standard station. The photo just allows us to see how the awning supports actually extend over a flat-roofed main building.   LENS OF SUTTON

provided at Lambourn, Winscombe and Cowley (Uxbridge Vine Street branch) and Uxbridge High Street, although in this latter case the station was of timber rather than brick construction.

The patterns described so far cover the principal types of station built by the GWR. However, a significant number of station buildings were not designed by the company engineers but by independent contractors working either for lines which were subsequently absorbed or, occasionally, on projects promoted by the GWR. Some of these engineers were sufficiently successful to be employed on a number of railway projects, with the result that their station designs recur at several locations. Others appear to have enjoyed more localised employment so that their style of building may only be found along a single line. Let us look at some examples.

One of the most successful of the independent engineers was William Clarke. He was employed on many projects between about 1859 and 1890, including no less than ten branch and secondary routes which became the property of the Great Western. Amongst these were the Kingsbridge, Bridport and Abbotsbury branches; the Bristol and North Somerset line including the branch to Camerton; and several lines in the Welsh border country, including the Kington branch. At least 24 stations may be confidently attributed to Clarke.

Their architectural style was both distinctive and pleasing. They were commonly, though not exclusively, built in brick with stone quoins and reveals. The gable ends, which were capped with a flat

Two views of one of William Clarke's lovely stations at Presteign in the Welsh borders. A closer view of the goods shed appears on page 17.   COLLECTION MIKE LLOYD
and L & GRP, COURTESY DAVID & CHARLES

Jackson's book on the Abbotsbury branch
(see Appendix).

A less decorative, but still very satisfy-
ing style of building, was the standard
station provided on the Didcot, Newbury
and Southampton line. This design is
another personal favourite and provides
excellent illustration of how a particular
style was associated with an individual
line. These station buildings looked more
like houses than railway structures and it
comes as no surprise to find that several
have survived as private dwellings. They
did, of course, provide accommodation as
well as functioning as the main office for
the station, which partly explains their
'domestic' appearance. But with their tiled
canopies, dormer windows, decorative
bargeboards and sloping-roofed extensions, they looked for all the world like
Victorian villas. In all, eight stations were
built in this style, by whom I am not
certain. The engineer for the DN & S was
John Fowler but whether he was responsible for the design of these structures, I
have not been able to clarify.

Stations on the Exe Valley line similarly
show a strong family likeness. This route

Platform and roadside views of the standard DN & S station house, Litchfield (upper) and Whitchurch (lower). It is no surprise that several of these structures have survived to the present as private houses.   COURTESY GILBERT LUDLOW and E. FRANKLIN

began as an independent venture sponsored by two companies but financial difficulties saw the GWR take over long before the lines were finished. However, contracts for the main stations had already been let to one W. B. Berry of Crediton, an arrangement the GWR was seemingly prepared to honour. The result was chalet-style buildings of almost identical format at Cadeleigh, Up Exe, Thorverton and Brampford Speke and a very similar pattern at Bampton built by another contractor, Nathaniel Fogg. Stoutly built in local stone, with twin gables facing the platform and decorative bargeboards, these were quite unlike standard Great Western structures, but very attractive nonetheless.

Of course, many independent lines were noted more for the modesty of their buildings than for the stylish designs of men like Clarke. A good example of simpler and cheaper buildings were those created by Arthur Pain. He engineered several lines around the country but in Great Western territory was responsible for the Highworth branch in Wiltshire and the Culm Valley line in East Devon.

Pain's quite unpretentious buildings were brick-built on the Culm Valley line but of timber construction on the branch to Highworth. The brick stations usually incorporated a visible framework of timbers which might be considered attractive, depending on your taste! However, the overall style in both cases was very similar, with a steeply pitched roof surmounting a plain and purely functional building. The canopies, where present, lacked any sort of decoration and could not have afforded generous protection against the elements.

Amongst the many lines in Wales absorbed at the grouping, there was so much variety as to defy succinct summary. My recollections of the ex-Taff Vale stations are, with certain exceptions, of squat, plain buildings, often built of the dark Pennant sandstone which lies like a mantle across the South Wales coalfield. Cream bricks provided contrast at the quoins and reveals. Treherbert, Dinas and Maerdy come to mind as examples of this unassuming style. Simple timber buildings were widely used too, occasionally with the planking arranged to produce geometric patterns as at Ynishir, but most commonly as plain, vertical planking as at Abertwsswg, which was a Brecon and Merthyr line station.

The characteristic Exe Valley station at Cadeleigh.　　　LENS OF SUTTON

Apart from the contrast in materials, there are clear stylistic similarities in these two buildings by Arthur Pain. The brick structure (above) is Uffculme on the Culm Valley Railway whilst the timber building is Hannington on the High-worth branch.
J. H. MOSS and C. GORDON WATFORD

Two common styles of Taff Vale Railway buildings. The upper view of Ynishir shows a timber structure with its 'herring-bone' pattern in the planking whilst below, the station at Ynysybwl was a blend of brick and stone.
HMRS and W. A. CAMWELL

Timber was widely used in west Wales too. Many of the stations on the Manchester and Milford line, for example, were modest wooden structures, although larger stations such as Lampeter merited more substantial, though still plain, stone buildings. In Pembrokeshire, the branch from Whitland to Pembroke Dock possessed some lovely structures in stone, particularly at Pembroke Dock itself and Tenby, where the station was further enhanced by an unusually ornamented valance to the platform canopy.

Space precludes a more detailed review of main station buildings, particularly those of the independent railways where there was such a lot of variety. If this glimpse of the medley of styles has provided even a partial indication of the scope, then it has achieved its primary objective. Let's move on to other buildings in the scene.

A simple timber building on the Brecon & Merthyr Railway at Abertwsswg. The low platform and shelter in the middle distance is probably a colliers' platform served only by workmen's trains, one of which may be standing on a siding beyond. The photo was taken in 1922.   HMRS

Tenby, photographed c.1911 and showing the unusually ornamented platform canopies.   G. M. PERKINS

GOODS SHEDS AND ENGINE SHEDS

Whilst station buildings and signal boxes (see later) have been the subject of systematic study, goods and engine sheds seem to have escaped detailed chronological examination. Needless to say, though, any attempt to piece together the story must start with Brunel.

The Brunel goods sheds, and their 'offspring', were handsome buildings and it is so typical of the GWR that a purely functional building should be stylish. Brunel's sheds were built in brick, stone or timber but always to an identifiable overall design. Characteristically they possessed wide, low pitched roofs and end walls which were pierced with a pair of arches, one for the line and one for the road vehicles. Interposed between the arches at one end there would usually be a lean-to office with a sloping roof and a chimney which often emerged through the apex of the main shed roof. Sometimes the door and window arches had a Gothic shape to match the style of Brunel's mock-Tudor stations, on other occasions the vehicle arches were round and the windows were simple rectangles. A nice example of the 'Gothic' style, in brick and stone, was pro-

The goods shed at Hatch, functional but also very stylish. The circular end window was not a normal feature.   LENS OF SUTTON

vided at Henley and a fine 4 mm scale model of a similar shed from Culham was described by Bob Logan in *Model Railway Journal* No. 21. The simpler style was exemplified at Hatch on the Chard branch.

By the 1860s, new designs for small sheds had been evolved from Brunel's patterns. These were typically in brick but

the road and rail arches were timber clad, sometimes with vertical planking, on other occasions horizontal. The sheds at Thame and Bourne End appeared to be in this style, so too the one at Newnham in Gloucestershire. Marlow was a close relative although it was altered in later life and also had windows in the end wall,

A classic Brunelian goods shed at Penryn, complete with the external office placed between the end arches.
L & GRP, CTY.
DAVID & CHARLES

Marlow (left) and Abingdon (below) both show the 'family features' but also have detailed variations which make them distinctive.

AUTHOR'S
COLLECTION

Faringdon, seen here in its final days, had a shed very similar in style to Penryn but modified by the addition of road canopies and a corrugated iron extension, although the latter is not visible in this view. In some records the shed is attributed to Brunel, although this is unlikely. J. H. MOSS

which was not usual. The shed at Faringdon could be considered as a stone version
of the same basic design, although it was
a little earlier than the other examples.
Abingdon was something of a hybrid,
clearly 'Brunelian' in origin, but, whilst
one end had the timber-clad framing over
the arch, the other end was entirely
timber-clad.

Towards the end of the 19th century,
two standard styles emerged. Both were
usually executed in brick with recessed
panels on the main walls, pierced with tall
windows of either arched or rectangular
format. Road access was through bays in
the side rather than the end walls. The first
type had a trio of arched windows set in
the gable end. Adrian Vaughan's book
provides excellent official plans of sheds to
this design intended for Risca and Tenby
in South Wales. The second type, which
is only really a variation, saw the three
windows replaced by a more extensive
area of glazing which sometimes filled the
gable end. I recall, with pleasure, spending
a spring morning in 1989 recording a surviving shed in this style at Brent and I
believe the old shed at Tetbury is also still
in use.

The Great Western also possessed
several designs of shed where the goods

*A new standard shed at Yealmpton. Sheds in this (and a similar) style, seem to have appeared in
the 1890s.*   AUTHOR'S COLLECTION

The alternative standard goods shed from the 1890s with its gable end glazing. This example is at Tetbury.   A. ATTEWELL

road ran alongside the shed rather than through it, the loading area being protected by a side awning or canopy. Rather austere designs of this general type were provided at Culkerton, Cardigan, Coleford and Princetown. I'm not sure whether we can refer to these as a 'standard' style but they certainly occurred across the system.

The independent railways that were later absorbed had their own styles of goods shed and some were rather fine. William Clarke, for instance, was quite capable of matching his lovely station buildings with functional but still elegantly finished sheds. Fencote on the Bromyard line and Gara Bridge on the Kingsbridge line were examples. The Exe

Two examples at Coleford (top) and Culkerton (below) of a lineside design of the 1880s. Further examples could also be found at Cardigan (see Part 1, pp. 55 & 57) and Princetown. The need for this particular design is unclear although they may have been intended for narrow or confined sites in which the wider standard sheds would not easily fit, or they may have just been cheaper to build.

L & GRP, COURTESY DAVID & CHARLES and TONY DYER

Contrasting designs of goods sheds on independent lines. Presteign (top) possessed a shed by William Clarke. The timber shed at Uffculme (centre) was by Arthur Pain and was similar to others provided by the same engineer on the Highworth branch. Hampstead Norris (bottom) had one of the standard Didcot, Newbury & Southampton line sheds, simple and quite plain and, in comparison with the rather stylish stations on the line, a little disappointing.
J. H. MOSS, LENS OF SUTTON and L & GRP, CTY. DAVID & CHARLES

Two interior views of goods sheds which I hope will be of value to modellers. In the upper photograph staff are using the crane to load a small cart, whilst the lower picture illustrates a vehicle bay. Note the simple loading gauge suspended from the roof timbers.

AUTHOR'S
COLLECTION
and A. ATTEWELL

Valley stations, which we considered a little earlier, possessed solid goods sheds built in local stone to match the main buildings, enlivened with nice detail such as the circular windows in the end wall, the deep bargeboarding and the ornamental ridge tiles.

In contrast, others are disappointing. I have never liked the plain and 'boxy' Didcot, Newbury & Southampton line sheds, nor the timber examples supplied by Arthur Pain to the Highworth and Culm lines, sheds in the worst sense of the word. Perhaps they help to remind that these goods facilities were, first and foremost, working premises in which delicate ridge tiles and bold fenestration were purely cosmetic. But although architecturally of little merit, in the context of this book we should note that they are not untypical of smaller branch line practice.

After the First World War, some branch goods sheds required replacement. By this stage, the economic realities of railway operation meant that the substantial sheds that the Victorians had favoured were unlikely to be replicated. Instead, utilitarian structures in corrugated iron appeared on the scene. Appropriate to traffic needs, yes – but aesthetically pleas-

ing, no! Blenheim and Woodstock was one branch station 'favoured' with one of these sheds.

Internal features in goods sheds are not to be overlooked in making our models. The large windows and vehicle access points make the interior, or parts of it, easily visible. A normal arrangement would be for a platform, often of wood, to run the length of the shed so that goods could be off-loaded from wagons at any

point. On the road side, vehicle bays would be let into the platform to facilitate easy transhipment to carts or lorries. There would usually be a crane which would often be built into the timber framing of the roof rather than being free-standing. When the shed lacked one of the characteristic office extensions, then an office area within a corner would be screened off with wooden partitions. Roof timbers were substantial and sometimes elaborate, but

Two views of the substantial goods shed at Bodmin. Note the mobile scales on the left of the interior view.   P. J. GARLAND

The new engine shed at Treherbert, photographed in 1925. Shed facilities of this scale were, of course, rare on branch lines and usually reflected special circumstances. In this case, the extensive Rhondda coal traffic justified the fleet of 56XX and 66XX class engines and their servicing facilities.
THE WELSH INDUSTRIAL AND MARITIME MUSEUM

A more usual size of branch shed at Tetbury. This style of building was replicated at a number of locations (with minor variations) and could be considered as a standard design.
J. H. RUSSELL

whether they would be seen in detail within a model is open to question.

In comparison to the goods shed, the branch line engine shed was relatively rare and became rarer through time as many were closed long before the lines themselves disappeared, engines being supplied from larger sheds within the division. It is harder, therefore, to identify distinctive styles. Dean and Churchward developed standard engine sheds which were used at major depots, but since these bore no relation to the needs of branches, they had little or no influence upon styles of building on these lines.

The common characteristic which branch sheds almost always shared was that they were single track facilities, built to house one or, at most, two engines. Building materials were brick and/or stone but not usually timber. Some corrugated iron sheds were provided, for example at Pontrilas for the Golden Valley line and at Woodstock. In some locations the engine sheds appear to have been matched to styles used on other buildings at the site, particularly the goods shed. The little

The sheds at Moretonhampstead (top) and St. Ives (above) show clear similarities in style. Both were originally built for broad gauge engines. The signal box attached to the Moretonhampstead shed was one of those oddities which were typical of branch lines and made them so characterful.
W. A. CAMWELL

stone shed at Faringdon was in a matching stone and deployed an almost identical style of window to the goods shed. At Tetbury, the recessed brick panels which were a feature of the standard GWR goods shed were also mirrored in the engine shed, although here the windows were different. The engine shed at Wallingford, which dated from the same period as the one at Tetbury, was stylistically the same and, as far as it is possible, could be considered a standard design.

Sometimes more unusual designs occurred. My favourite example here is Moretonhampstead where the lofty engine shed, originally designed for a broad gauge engine and bearing strong similarities to sheds at Ashburton and St. Ives, sprouted a signal box from its side wall. Much Wenlock was another oddity, although quite charming. Like Tetbury, it incorporated a water tower as a part of its overall structure but the brickwork, on most sheds usually plain to the point of being dull, was here enlivened with col-

Further examples of branch sheds. The timber shed at Minehead (top left) started life down the line at Watchet and was moved in 1874 when the branch was extended to Minehead. It was photographed c.1937. The rather more substantial double road shed at Newquay (bottom left) is in a style used at a number of locations around the early 1900s. The small shed (top right) with the decorative brickwork stood at Shipston on Stour, whilst the photograph (above) provides a glimpse of Abingdon shed and its associated facilities.

W. A. CAMWELL, J. H. RUSSELL and R. C. RILEY

The interior of Bodmin engine shed provides more detail that should interest the modelmaker. The large, wall-mounted gas lamps are particularly prominent, but there are many other features to study.
P. J. GARLAND

A rare view of the yard at Much Wenlock with the rear of the engine shed and the goods shed beyond, in the left centre. The branch train seems to be undergoing its weekly clean. The large loading bank is interesting with coal and some impressive pieces of timber awaiting removal.

C. L. MOWAT

Much Wenlock engine shed, with its dentilations and decorative brickwork.

J. H. MOSS

2—4—0 'Large Metro' tank, No. 3592 inside Newcastle Emlyn shed.   COLLECTION P. KARAU

The exterior view of Newcastle Emlyn shed shows the building to have been, architecturally, of less merit than some of the other examples illustrated! However, modest structures like this were quite common on branches.
W. A. CAMWELL

Just to complete this look at Newcastle Emlyn, we have included another picture of the station taken on the same occasion when the branch engine, Collett 0–4–2T No. 5819, was waiting with a departure to Pencader on a typically wet West Wales day. The train was probably comprised of a 70ft concertina ex-slip coach which was used on the line in its latter days.
W. A. CAMWELL

Helston station with a good example of a 'Type 3' signal box. (For further views of this interesting station, see Part 1, pages 51–53.)
R. S. CARPENTER

oured quoins and dentilations around the eaves and in the gable over the main doors.

SIGNAL BOXES

Signal boxes have always appealed to me as fascinating places and although I have never had the pleasure of entering a working box, as a trainspotter I liked to position myself near a signal box, listening for the tell-tale beats on the bells, watching the shadowy movements of the signalman and then scanning the scene to see which signals had been operated.

Architecturally they were often fine structures, with enough decoration to lift them out of the purely functional pattern into which they might otherwise so readily lapse. Great Western boxes were, in truth, much plainer than many of those of other companies and contractors but they were very distinctive, and later designs, in particular, were immediately recognisable as belonging to the GWR.

The GWR built signal boxes throughout most of its history, certainly from about 1870 onwards. Over the following 70 years, many different designs and variations were introduced, so that the complete history of signal box development on the GWR is lengthy and complex. We are fortunate, therefore, that the course of signal box development has been set out most clearly and fully by John Morris and Reg Instone. Since their work has been published in several sources, there seems little point in repeating their findings in full. So I have tried to provide a summary (*Table 1*) which sets out basic descriptions of the main types that are likely to be

relevant to branch line modellers. Sources which provide a full account are given in the Appendix.

The essential points to observe from *Table 1* are that first, most styles could be built as either brick with timber framing or, as all-timber boxes whilst secondly, certain of these designs were clearly

evolved from earlier models. The most abrupt change of style comes with the introduction of the Type 7 box and its numerous offspring. It may also be observed that different styles tended to overlap rather than occupy discrete time periods. Thus, for example, Type 5 boxes were known to have been built as late as

Table 1.   Summary of Main Styles of GWR Signal Boxes

Type	Main distinguishing features	Dates built
1	Entirely brick-built with gabled roof. Sliding windows two panes wide, three deep. Rare on branch lines	Early 1870s
2	Brick base with timber upper – vertical boarding (some all timber, Type 22). Windows three panes deep and either 3 or 4 panes wide. Hipped Roof	1875–80
3	Brick base with timber upper – vertical boarding (a few all timber, Type 23), but gabled rather than hipped roof. Gable vents have seven louvres. Windows as Type 2 but more usually 4 panes wide rather than 3. Common on branches in southern part of system	1880s
4	Brick base with timber upper – horizontal boarding, gabled roof with finials. Gable vents have four louvres. Windows as Type 2 and 3. Variations of this type (4b and 4c) possess external porches. Mostly in northern part of system	Mid 1880s
5	Mainly of brick construction with small areas of horizontal timber boarding (some all timber, Type 25). Gabled roof of lower pitch than Type 4, with louvres. Windows as in Types 2, 3, and 4. Finials and ridge vents (first use). First GWR box to be used throughout the system, very common on branches	Approx 1890–1902
6	Smaller version (narrower) of Type 5, often built on platforms and quite widely used on branches	As Type 5
7/27	Built in very large numbers as both brick (Type 7) and timber (Type 27) and subject to many variations. Operating room windows divided to provide 3 upper panes and 2 lower panes. Prominent eaves brackets, hipped roof with finials and vents. Some had internal stairs replacing external wooden steps	1896–1925
8/28	Gabled version of Type 7/27 showing only small detailed differences. Timber boxes (Type 28) were more numerous than brick boxes (Type 8)	1921–1933

Source:– Compiled from The Signalling Study Group *The Signal Box* (OPC) pp. 160–164 and 224–226.

Left: *Coleford signal box doesn't fit too neatly into the typology in Table 1, but perhaps represents a platform version of the 'Type 3'.* Right: *Eynsham signal box, one of the smaller 'Type 6' boxes designed particularly for branch stations where space was often at a premium.*

LENS OF SUTTON and J. H. RUSSELL

A 'Type 5' signal box at Cirencester. Boxes of this style were widely used on the GWR and were possibly the most common type on branch and secondary routes.

J. H. RUSSELL

1902, at least 6 years after the first Type 7 boxes were introduced.

At the risk of making an unhelpfully sweeping statement, all of these main types could be found on branch lines at one time or another, so if you are a modeller inventing a location, you could almost take your pick. Some of the later styles (e.g. Type 7) were larger than earlier designs (e.g. Type 3) and you would need to be sure that your layout required a box of that capacity. But there is still a lot of scope for variety.

Having said that, some designs were far more widespread on branches than others. I conducted a small photo survey of some 60 branch stations where I was able to identify the style of the signal box and although I found examples of all types except 1, 2/22 and 24, the largest group were the Type 5 boxes (accounting for almost a third of my sample), followed by Type 7 designs. Many of the Type 7 boxes were replacements for older boxes as occurred, for example, at Camerton. Introduction of the Type 5 box coincided with a period in which the Great Western was apparently engaged upon a drive to complete its programme of interlocking. As Table 1 also notes, it was the first box to be used as a standard throughout the system and these two facts taken together, help to account for the widespread incidence of this style. Examples of Type 5 boxes were located at Henley, Tavistock and Yelverton, whilst Type 7 designs were provided at Wargrave, Lampeter, Dunkerton and Tiverton and Type 27 (the all-timber version) at Marlow. After the Type 5 and 7 designs, the next most common style was the Type 3 with nice examples at, amongst other locations, Helston, Abingdon and Martock.

Alongside the GWR's own designs were a large number of signal boxes which were acquired when independent lines were taken into the company's ownership. Some were boxes designed by the independent railways themselves but most were supplied by signalling contractors, particularly McKenzie and Holland, Saxby and Farmer and the Gloucester Carriage & Wagon Company.

Most of the McKenzie and Holland boxes in Great Western ownership were to be found in South Wales and on lines in the northern part of the system. Typically they were of brick (or stone) and timber construction with horizontal weatherboarding and six paned windows. From

Three 20th century boxes. Wargrave (top) was of the 'Type 7' design whilst Luxulyan (centre) was a timber version of the same style ('Type 27'). In the lower view, a 'Type 28' box at Newent is shown.
P. MOFFATT
A. ATTEWELL
and L. E. COPELAND

my youth, I can also recall the special design provided for the Taff Vale Railway which had the additional features of shaped and pierced bargeboards and decorative ridge tiles.

Saxby and Farmer were more widely used in the south of the network and since they seem to have been less heavily involved in South Wales, fewer of their boxes became GWR property. Those that did shared several common design features. Boxes were often almost square in ground plan and the hipped roof gave little or nothing in the way of a ridge. The lower part of the box would often be brick, usually with a single window to illuminate the locking room, whilst the operating floor was encased in a stout timber frame with horizontal weatherboarding. Some, for example the boxes at Clevedon and Cheddar, possessed elongated 'toplights' above the main windows whilst others, for example those supplied to the Didcot, Newbury & Southampton line, did not.

Saxby and Farmer provided boxes for the southern part of the DN & S, the northern section between Didcot and Newbury being built using Gloucester Carriage & Wagon boxes. These, too, were timber-framed structures on a brick base, but the Gloucester boxes had gabled rather than hipped roofs with decorated and pierced bargeboards. Windows were

divided into four panes, as, incidentally, were the Saxby and Farmer designs. The Midland and South Western Junction Railway also made some use of the Gloucester company and another contractor, Evans O'Donnell.

In presenting what is no more than a 'thumb-nail' sketch of signal box develop-

ment, I am conscious of concealing a lot of detailed variation. I do urge interested readers to refer to more specialised sources for a fuller picture. My purpose here is simply to indicate, once again, the range and variety that could be a part of the Great Western branch line scene and to try to highlight the styles that were typical.

Three common styles of contractors' signal boxes. Cardigan box was built to one of McKenzie and Holland's standard designs. Compton (bottom left) was equipped with a Gloucester Carriage & Wagon box, whilst Clevedon had one of the Saxby & Farmer boxes, with its distinctive window 'toplights'.
P. J. GARLAND, E. WILMSHURST and J. M. HODGETTS

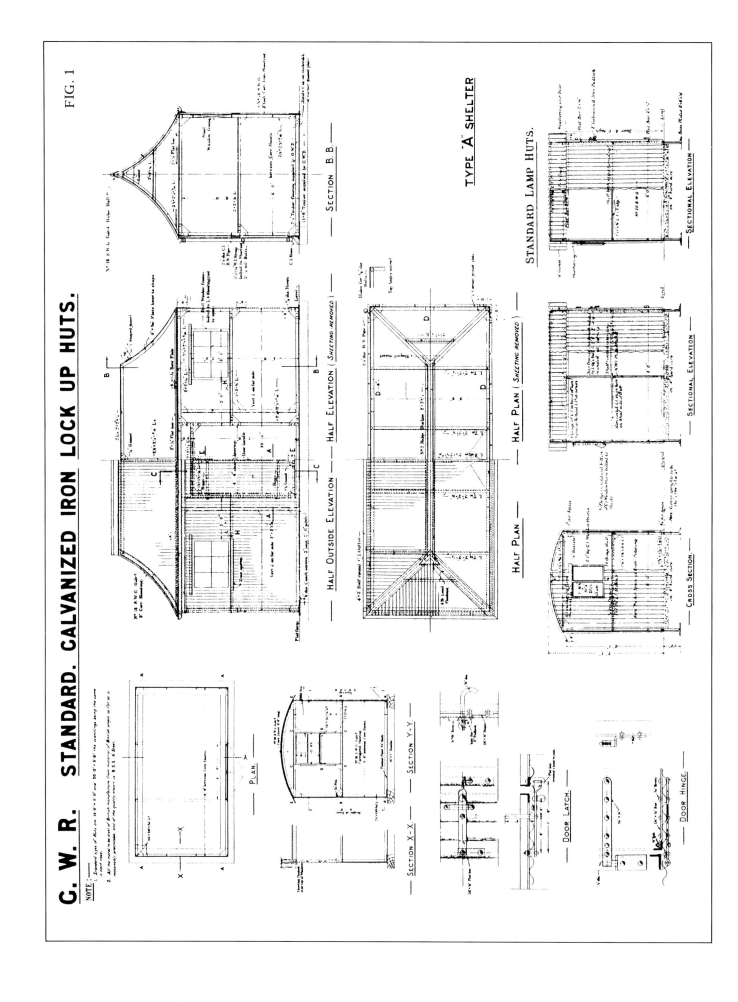

G. W. R. STANDARD. GALVANIZED IRON LOCK UP HUTS.

FIG. 1

TYPE "A" SHELTER

STANDARD LAMP HUTS.

CHAPTER TWO

MINOR STRUCTURES, FIXTURES AND FITTINGS

A beautiful example of the standard halt at Rollright on the Banbury & Cheltenham line. With the exception of the end ramp battens, all the standard features are illustrated. This was one of the more interesting halts with a separate goods yard which is just discernible in the distance.
J. H. RUSSELL

IN the very early years of the 20th century, the GWR began to develop its fleet of railmotors and, in order to optimise the use of these vehicles, provided a large number of new halts on both branches and main lines. Coming at the peak of the Great Western's drive towards standardisation, it is no surprise to find that many conformed to an identical format.

Platforms were usually of timber construction with 12 in × 3 in planks laid parallel to the track. These were supported on cross-braced timber legs of robust construction. Uprights measured 6 in × 6 in with struts and braces 4 in × 3 in. To the rear of the normally narrow platform (minimum width 7 ft) was a post and rail fence, 4 ft high. This might be either a single top rail with strands of galvanised wire beneath, or three further planks equally spaced between the top rail and the platform. From photo evidence, wire was more usual. The platform end ramps had thin, transverse battens, equally spaced down the ramp, to provide footholds.

Shelter was provided by either a simple wooden structure or one of the company's corrugated iron 'pagodas', officially a 'Type A' shed. These distinctive buildings (*Fig. 1*) derived their name from the curving roof which imparted a vaguely oriental quality to the design. (Why anyone would wish to embellish a tin shed with a Chinese style roof escapes me!). *Fig. 1* shows a pagoda with windows but designs without windows were also used.

In some cases, lighting for halts was provided by a set of standard gas lamps but often one or two Tilley lamps (see page 57) would be all there was to illuminate the scene. Standard gas lamps might be mounted on cast iron columns according to normal practice but many halts had their lamps supported on a stout timber

Another halt, also on the Banbury & Cheltenham line, in this case illustrating nicely the battens fixed to the ramp to provide footholds.
FRANK PACKER

Footbridges were, in practice, subject to substantial detail variations. These four illustrations reveal some of the possible combinations. The two photographs on the left show the lattice design in use at Bridgnorth (top) and Hallatrow (bottom), although in the example at Bridgnorth the footway was open to the elements. Note that at Hallatrow, the area beneath the supports has been enclosed to create lock-ups. On the right the steel-plated design is illustrated. Thame (top) is virtually a standard bridge whilst Yelverton (bottom) sports a slightly more elaborate valance, angle rather than column supports, and timber panels on the stairs in lieu of the more normal steel plate.

W. A. CAMWELL, A. ATTEWELL and ROYE ENGLAND

attached to the top of the post and rail fence.

SHEDS AND LOCK-UPS

Pagoda sheds were not confined to use as waiting shelters on halts, since they appeared in very large numbers on stations where more substantial buildings formed the main station complex. Their roles in these situations could be very varied, perhaps acting as parcels offices, general stores, lamp rooms, lock-ups for equipment or even bicycle sheds.

There were also smaller sheds available for similar functions, again constructed in corrugated iron, but this time with a simple curved roof in place of the more fanciful pagoda. These lock-ups usually had a single, small end window and measured either 14 ft × 8 ft or 20 ft × 8 ft in plan. Smaller still were the standard lamp huts, usually no more than 8 ft × 6 ft and, as their name implies, normally used for the storage and servicing of lamps.

As buildings which were cheap and easy to provide, branch stations which required some expansion of facilities would tend to acquire these sheds and lock-ups. This often took place in an incremental fashion so that little corrugated 'colonies' of sheds would be established in and around the station. Look at Wallingford, for example, and you will see what I mean! This was a typical feature that lent character to the branch line scene and which can be effective and interesting within a model.

FOOTBRIDGES

On true branch lines, footbridges were a comparative rarity. As Chapter 2 in Part I sought to demonstrate, the majority of branch stations were of a single track– single platform format, in which the need for a footbridge obviously did not arise. Even when two platforms were created through the construction of passing loops, footbridges were not automatically provided, unless it was awkward for passengers to get from one side to the other. However, there were sufficient examples on branches and secondary lines to make passing reference worthwhile.

If we set aside detailed variations and the occasional experimental designs which inevitably occurred on a system as extensive as the Great Western, we can summarise standard footbridges as falling into one of two categories. In the first design, which was much more numerous, the steps from the landing and the section

across the tracks were enclosed to a height of about 4 ft 6 in with steel plates. The basic framework was of steel angle. The main supports might be on cast columns but could also be steel angle, in this latter instance often enclosed in timber. The main stairs down to the platform might be similarly enclosed, in either timber or steel plate, though some sported cast balusters. The second design employed the same basic framework but the steel panels were substituted with an open pattern of lattice work made up of steel strip. Examples of the steel plated design stood

at Thame, Yelverton and Tavistock whilst a superb example of the lattice work bridge was in use at Dulverton, at the north end of the Exe Valley line.

Both types could be supplied without roofs although it was more usual to find some form of protection from the elements. The roof itself was nothing more than corrugated iron but the eye would usually be distracted by the splendid valancing which adorned these bridges. There were different designs of valance but most were similar to Great Western platform canopy valance, with a saw-

Two examples of the manner in which the railway's corrugated sheds would often congregate into little 'colonies' in and around the station. The upper view is of Abingdon whilst below is Wallingford. The view of Wallingford affords clear illustration of the difference in size between the standard lock-ups (right) and the smaller lamp huts (left).
L & GRP, CTY. DAVID & CHARLES and LENS OF SUTTON

Goods yards would usually have a weighbridge and office. The office always had a window onto the bridge plate, a chimney and a door in the end wall but although this configuration was repeated at dozens of locations, there was quite a lot of variation in the details of design. Brick structures were usual but stone and timber offices were also in use. Those illustrated were at Shipston on Stour, Presteign, Yealmpton, Chipping Norton and an unidentified location at which Weedon Brothers, coal merchants, had a depot – perhaps even an early view at Wallingford before the yard was enlarged?
M. E. J. DEANE, J. H. MOSS, E. T. DAY, A. ATTEWELL and COLLECTION P. KARAU

Llanfyllin, showing the yard. Trade in livestock was quite important on this branch and this is reflected in the provision of several pens and a loading bank. A closer view of the goods shed is provided in Part 1, page 30.

SPEIGHT FAMILY COLLECTION

Coal was commonly weighed and bagged direct from the wagon. The scales used to weigh the coal are shown here.

A. ATTEWELL

The goods yard at Lechlade in 1947 with some characteristic features and activities. In the upper view, 0-6-0 pannier tank No. 1742 was shunting the yard whilst in the bottom photograph, bagged maize was being offloaded onto one of the company's lorries. Many branch yards utilised disused vehicles for storage and the middle photograph features two rather sorry grounded 40ft passenger brake vans flanking the goods shed.

J. H. RUSSELL

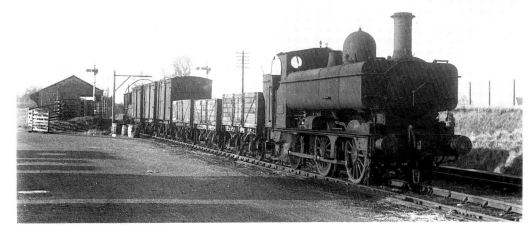

More details of a branch goods yard. This example is at Kington where the old terminus was used as a goods yard. Note the number of 'foreign' wagons in the sidings.
C. L. MOWAT

Two examples of light yard cranes at Wrington (above) and Bourne End (right). Some yards were equipped with a heavier version of the design shown at Bourne End, capable of lifting up to six tons.
IAN BAKER and A. ATTEWELL

A loading gauge would always be provided in a yard and several different designs were in use. The example at Fairford (above) shows a common style of metal gauge whilst the right-hand view shows an earlier wooden-posted version at Malmesbury.

NRM and E. K. LOCKSTONE

Company stables dating from the turn of the century and illustrating the commonality of style. When horses gave way to motor vehicles, these buildings were often converted to garages by replacing one end wall with doors. These pictures show stables at Thame, Abingdon and Little Somerford respectively. Although Little Somerford is not a branch line station, the building is a standard structure similar to Thame. A. ATTEWELL

tooth pattern, pierced with pairs of holes arranged vertically.

LIVESTOCK FACILITIES

If we wander into the goods yard, apart from the goods shed itself, the other structures we might find would include cattle docks and stabling. It is easy to forget that the railway was, for most of its history, a major user of horses, and company stables were sometimes to be found at branch stations, especially termini. Standard designs were introduced at the end of the 19th century, usually in a style which matched the main station buildings of the period, with slate roofs and red brick work, reinforced with engineers' blue bricks. Abingdon provided a nice example.

Official drawings for standard cattle pens show wooden gates set within compounds that were sometimes also of timber construction but more commonly made from second-hand rail or signal rodding. Broad gauge bridge rail was frequently re-used in this way, especially on branches where cheap and improvised solutions to problems were more characteristic. Vertical lengths of rail were set in concrete to form supports to which horizontal pieces were bolted. Later designs employed concrete posts with round rodding to form the fencing (*Fig. 2*).

Rail-built cattle pens. Notice how bridge rail has been utilised for the horizontal bars but the vertical supports are old Vignoles (flat-bottomed) rail.   I. D. BEALE and A. ATTEWELL

The alternative (later) style of pen, with round bars set in concrete posts. Useful detail of the floor is also revealed, the pattern of raised bricks being designed to prevent the animals slipping. Notice, too, the provision for drinking water in the pens.
A. ATTEWELL

Floor areas might be chequered slabs and there would normally be a water trough and a drain. Standard arrangements show the rail immediately in front of the pens set in concrete with drainage gullies to facilitate cleansing. However, I should repeat the warnings against presumption that all branches necessarily followed standard practice. At Faringdon, for example, track alongside the pens possessed no special drainage and the pens themselves were of solid stone construction, like the rest of the station. Don't forget, if your modelling period is before about 1925, to make sure your pens are liberally daubed with the limewash which was used as a cleansing agent. After the mid 1920s, this practice was discontinued.

WATER TOWERS AND TANKS

Several different styles of small water tank were to be found on branch lines but two types were especially widespread. The more familiar and distinctively 'Great Western' was the conical-topped pillar tank. These large, cylindrical tanks were normally supported on a circular cast-iron column with an integral water crane. A steel ladder provided access to a small inspection hatch set in the conical 'lid'. (Incidentally, if you are modelling a tower and crane, or even the separate crane, don't forget the fire devil – the little stove with a tall chimney kept alongside the crane to tackle icing in winter.)

For locations where a larger capacity was required, water tanks would be pro-

G. W. R. STANDARD CATTLE PENS.

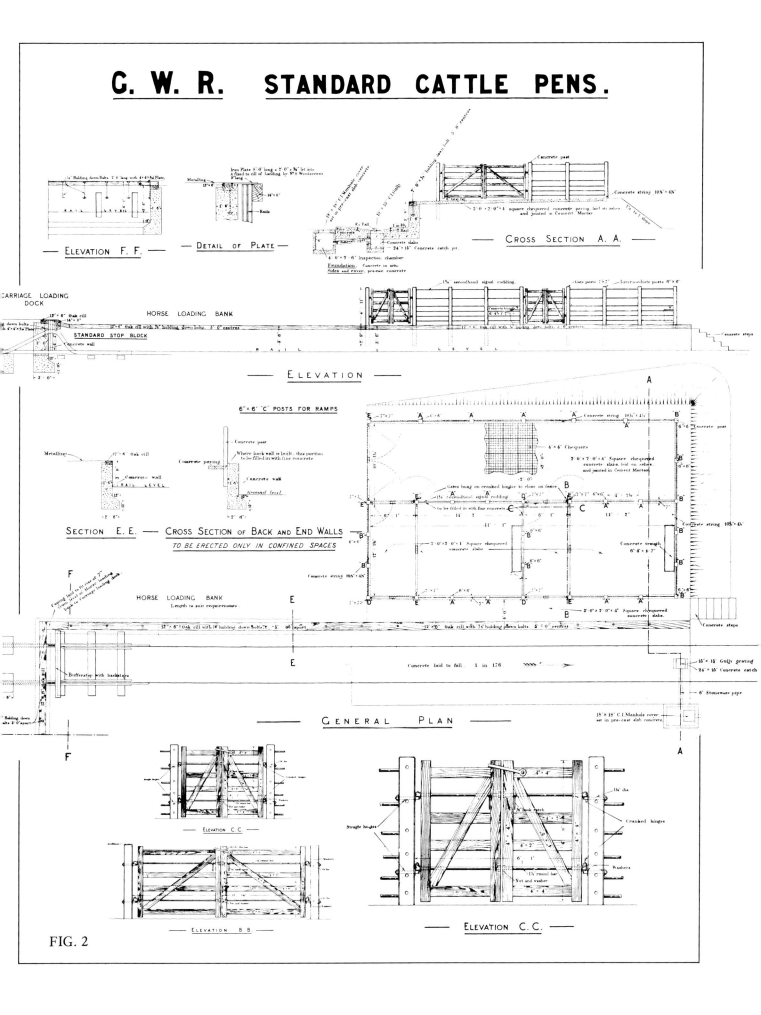

— ELEVATION F. F. —

— DETAIL OF PLATE —

CROSS SECTION A. A.

— ELEVATION —

6"×6" "C" POSTS FOR RAMPS

SECTION E. E. — CROSS SECTION of BACK and END WALLS
TO BE ERECTED ONLY IN CONFINED SPACES

HORSE LOADING BANK
Length to suit requirements.

GENERAL PLAN

— ELEVATION C. C. —

— ELEVATION B. B. —

— ELEVATION C. C. —

FIG. 2

Platform-mounted water crane at Witney.

R. E. JAMES-ROBERTSON

A standard conical pillar tank at Lambourn.   I. D. BEALE

vided. A common pattern comprised a rectangular tank supported on four, or sometimes six, cast-iron columns and often quite nicely finished. The columns usually had raised capitals from which sprang small brackets to support the tank. Between the tank itself and the columns, a narrow, cast-iron, pierced panel was added, which made the whole ensemble surprisingly decorative. The water crane was attached to the underside of the tank. Examples with six supporting columns stood at St. Ives, Chipping Norton and Clevedon, whilst Marlborough had one of the four-legged varieties. Some had integral coaling stages.

Variations on the theme were, of course, widespread. Faringdon possessed a raised tank alongside the engine shed, though in this case the cast pillars were replaced with solid stone walls at each end. Sometimes, especially on lines that had been inherited, the entire base of the tank would be walled. The tank at Blenheim had such a base and the example at Henley, built by a contractor, was also of a non-standard pattern.

The GWR had several designs for large tanks, including one where the tank was supported on square rather than round legs. But as far as I can establish from inspection of photos, these were confined to busier locations where there was a greater demand for water. The large com-

Minor Structures, Fixtures and Fittings

Three styles of rectangular water tank. The tanks at Marlborough (below left) and Clevedon (below right) share the decorative support panels, although the designs are actually different. Notice, also, that the Clevedon tank had round corners in contrast to the square corners used at Marlborough. The plainer style illustrated at the top is from Moreton-hampstead, but tanks of this type occurred widely on branches. I. D. BEALE, A. C. HAROLD and J. H. MOSS

bined tank and coaling stages of the type preserved at Didcot were also seldom to be seen on branches. Coaling was usually done from small wooden platforms alongside the shed or often, direct from wagons. Small hoists were occasionally used but many branch sheds saw engines coaled by hand.

FIXTURES AND FITTINGS

Although a correct balance of buildings is essential to creating a faithful model of a branch line scene, if we want to breathe life into that model, we should pay careful attention to the fixtures and fittings. The list is potentially endless so to try to keep this saga under some sort of control, a selective review of the more important is probably all that can reasonably be achieved here. But do inspect photos most carefully for small details that will improve your model.

Seats

Platform seats for all stations, not just branches, came in two basic styles, the second of which was subject to several variations. The oldest design in common usage was an all wooden seat, rather wide in relation to its height, with turned legs at the front and square legs at the back, and curved arm rests at each end. This was obviously a close relative of the standard waiting room seat, the main difference being that the seat used out-of-doors was not padded.

Chronologically it was followed by what most enthusiasts recognise as the standard platform seat of the GWR, in which the main support was provided by cast iron uprights which carried a narrower seat than the first design and two planks (separated) as the back rest. The variation in this design was provided with the casting which displayed the company's initials. Between their introduction in the early years of the 20th century and 1934, the casting showed the entwined insignia 'GWR'. After 1934, this was replaced by the angular 'shirt-button' monogram which was used on just about everything in the company's ownership for the next ten years. Seats in both styles survive in large numbers on British Rail today and are well known.

What is not so well known is that there was at least one other variation on this design. In the first decade of the century, the GWR conducted some experiments with new designs for the company's insignia. Some actually appeared on coaches

Early pattern platform seats, constructed from wood and normally with six legs, although as the example from Symonds Yat reveals (right), there was a four-legged version too. Close scrutiny of the seat at Bodmin (above) reveals the station name painted on the seat back, whilst the view at the foot of the page (also of Bodmin) shows one of the padded waiting room seats which has found its way onto the platform.
NATIONAL RAILWAY MUSEUM
and A. ATTEWELL

Later styles employed cast iron supports with the company's initials. The first design, introduced in the early years of the century employed the more elaborate monogram, illustrated in the view of Monmouth (top). After 1934, the simpler 'shirt-button' design was introduced (above). Occasionally, seats from independent companies survived in GWR ownership. The example (below left) at Mortonhampstead is thought to be from the South Devon Railway.

W. A. CAMWELL, L & GRP CTY. DAVID & CHARLES, and NATIONAL RAILWAY MUSEUM

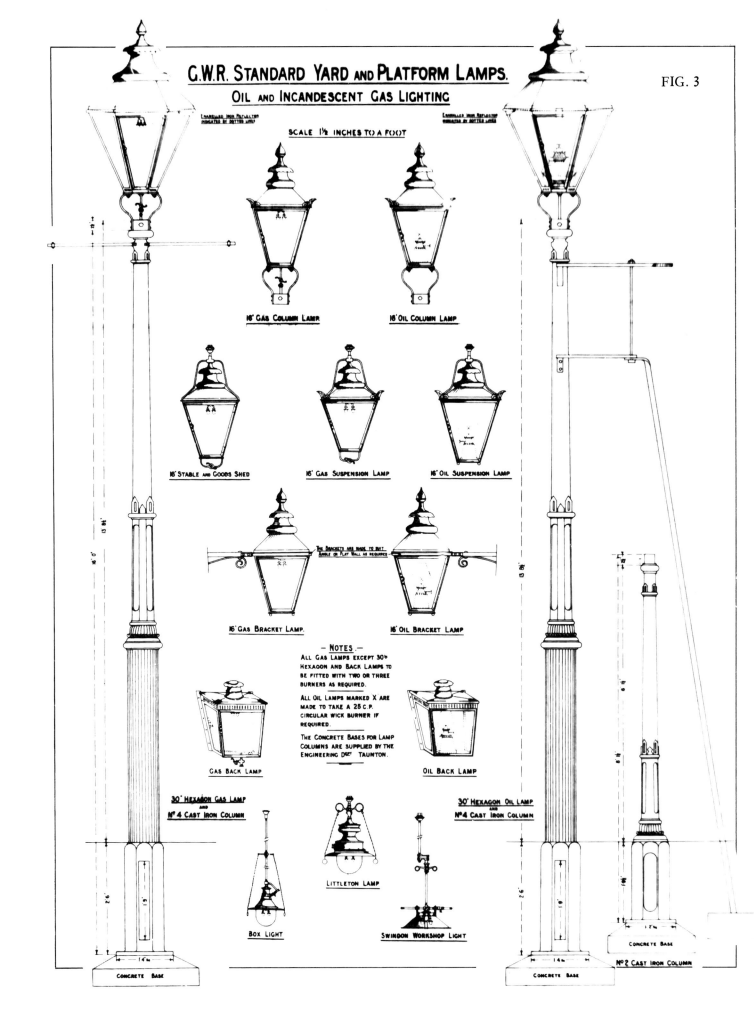

G.W.R. Standard Yard and Platform Lamps.

Oil and Incandescent Gas Lighting

FIG. 3

SCALE 1½ INCHES TO A FOOT

16' GAS COLUMN LAMP

16' OIL COLUMN LAMP

16' STABLE AND GOODS SHED

16' GAS SUSPENSION LAMP

16' OIL SUSPENSION LAMP

16' GAS BRACKET LAMP.

16' OIL BRACKET LAMP

— NOTES. —

ALL GAS LAMPS EXCEPT 30"
HEXAGON AND BACK LAMPS TO
BE FITTED WITH TWO OR THREE
BURNERS AS REQUIRED.

ALL OIL LAMPS MARKED X ARE
MADE TO TAKE A 25 C.P.
CIRCULAR WICK BURNER IF
REQUIRED.

THE CONCRETE BASES FOR LAMP
COLUMNS ARE SUPPLIED BY THE
ENGINEERING DEPT. TAUNTON.

GAS BACK LAMP

OIL BACK LAMP

30' HEXAGON GAS LAMP
AND
Nº 4 CAST IRON COLUMN

LITTLETON LAMP

30' HEXAGON OIL LAMP
AND
Nº 4 CAST IRON COLUMN

BOX LIGHT

SWINDON WORKSHOP LIGHT

CONCRETE BASE

CONCRETE BASE

CONCRETE BASE

Nº 2 CAST IRON COLUMN

Variations on a theme. Three examples of lamps for platform use, all similar but each one different. All employ the fluted column but the support for the lamp case differs on the lamp from Henley in Arden (left) and all three have contrasting styles of top case and chimney. The lamps from Symonds Yat and East Garston are both oil-lit.
NATIONAL RAILWAY MUSEUM and A. ATTEWELL

and there is evidence of seats being produced with experimental monograms too. My friend, David Hyde, photographed one at Kemble.

Unlike many other companies, the GWR did not make a habit of painting station names on seat backs. The HMRS actually go as far as to state in *Great Western Way* that 'no station names appeared on seats'. This is simply not true. It was not normal practice but around the period of the First World War at least, some branch stations certainly had seats with station names. Blenheim and Woodstock was a case in point and so was Faringdon.

Station Lamps

Station lamps almost represent a study in themselves, such was the variety of styles and possible combinations. First, there were several designs of cast-iron columns, including one which was fluted from base to top and seems to have been used for oil lamps, and another plainer design, which is recorded in official drawings as being for gas lights (*Figs 3 and 5*). To confuse matters further, these columns came in different lengths.

The lamps themselves were also subject to variation. Station lamps were square in horizontal section but tapered from top to base. The top casing concealed the chimney beneath several layers of ornamentation. Some of the designs were intended to be attached at their base to the

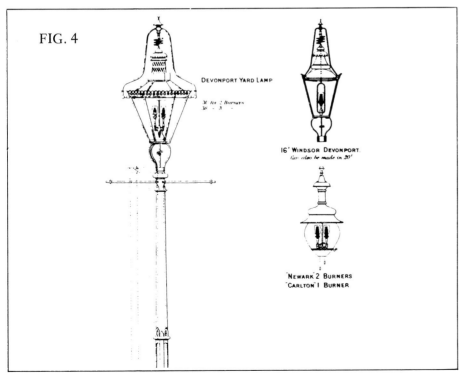

FIG. 4

DEVONPORT YARD LAMP

16' WINDSOR DEVONPORT

NEWARK 2 BURNERS
CARLTON 1 BURNER

A 16in gas column lamp at Wargrave.
DAVID HYDE

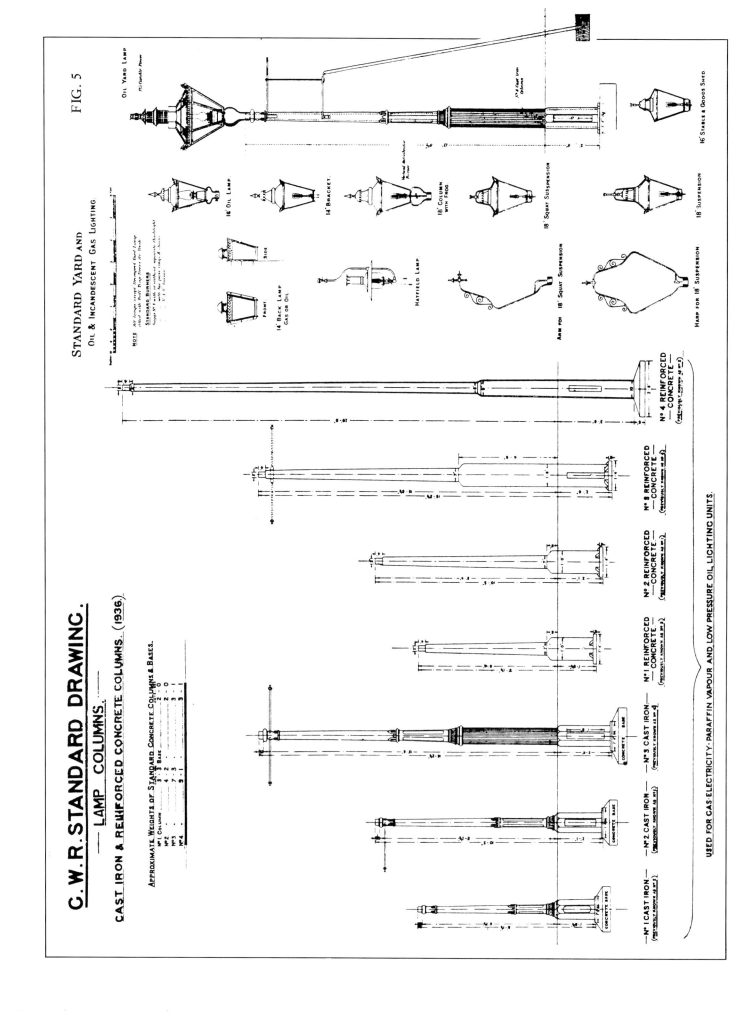

G.W.R. STANDARD DRAWING.

— LAMP COLUMNS. —

CAST IRON & REINFORCED CONCRETE COLUMNS. (1936.)

FIG. 5

STANDARD YARD AND
OIL & INCANDESCENT GAS LIGHTING.

USED FOR GAS·ELECTRICITY·PARAFFIN VAPOUR AND LOW PRESSURE OIL LIGHTING UNITS.

Left: *The taller (8ft 1½in) No. 2 cast column married to a standard 16in gas lamp (at Kingsbridge).* Centre: *The shorter (6ft 0½in) No. 1 column with a standard 16in oil lamp, a close-up of which is provided alongside (right).*
W. A. CAMWELL and A. ATTEWELL

Some lamps were suspended from ornamental brackets (referred to as 'harps' because of their shape). They could accommodate either 16in or 18in lamps. The lamp in the centre is one of the 'squat' suspension designs (see Fig. 5).
A. ATTEWELL

A standard yard lamp on a 14ft column at Cirencester.

J. H. RUSSELL

Examples of less common styles. The lamp cases from Woodstock (left) and Lambourn (second from left) are both standard GWR designs but the columns are atypical. The example from Bodmin (centre) is either not a GWR design at all, or represents a style that was not widely adopted. The fourth picture shows yet another variation with a standard lamp mounted on an extended column (Henley-on-Thames), whilst the last one shows a gas lamp case which appears at a number of GWR stations, but the origin of which has escaped me!
NATIONAL RAILWAY MUSEUM, L & GRP, CTY. DAVID & CHARLES, LENS OF SUTTON, PHOTOSCRIPT and A. ATTEWELL

Left: *Close-up of the support bracket and the gas feed apparatus.* Centre & right: *16in oil lamps mounted on plain concrete and wooden posts.*
A. ATTEWELL

Above & right: *Examples of the 'Littleton' gas lamp which was normally used inside stations or beneath canopies.*   A. ATTEWELL and NATIONAL RAILWAY MUSEUM

A 16in gas bracket lamp.
A. ATTEWELL

Left: *A 'Littleton' lamp attached to an external bracket.* Centre: *Plain gas lamps of this type feature in a number of views of branch stations but I have been unable to identify when they were introduced. Their lack of ornamentation suggests they might be a later style.* Right: *This lamp at Henley has the same design of head but is carried on a standard column fitted with an extension.*
A. ATTEWELL

LIGHTING STATIONS & HALTS

by

TILLEY LAMPS

BURN ORDINARY PARAFFIN (KEROSENE)

WIDELY USED TO-DAY BY THE G.W.R.

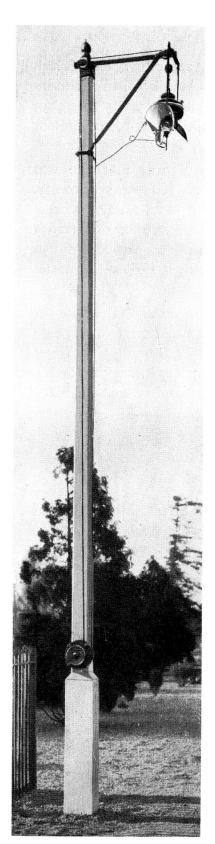

"CHALLOW" Lamp mounted on concrete column showing method of suspension and lowering gear.

There are innumerable stations and halts on Railways which are lighted by oil wick lamps of obsolete pattern, and as a result, these stations are dingy, dark and depressing. They can be transformed into brilliantly illuminated stations by installing Tilley Paraffin (Kerosene) Vapour Lamps. The psychological effect is very great and, as a result, traffic increases . . . .

The "Challow" pattern was specially designed to replace oil wick lamps at Challow Station on the G.W.R., and its use has been rapidly extended to other stations on this System. Is recommended for platform lighting, being the most efficient and economical form of lighting available. Mounted on concrete column so that the Lamp is suspended at a height of about 20 feet, the trough-shaped Reflector throws a beam of light 32 feet wide for a distance of 100 feet in each direction.

ONE TILLEY LAMP WILL REPLACE FIVE WICK LAMPS, YET EFFECT ECONOMY IN CONSUMPTION AND MAINTENANCE

Briefly, the station lighting is vastly improved, running costs and maintenance time are reduced and should electricity become available the concrete poles, lowering gear and "Radolux" reflectors may be readily adapted to electric lighting.

BRITISH MADE THROUGHOUT

*The photographs on this page show an installation of "CHALLOW" Lamps at **Aldermaston Station, Great Western Railway.** (Note the number of posts from which the ordinary oil lamp has been removed).*

THE TILLEY LAMP CO.
HENDON, N.W.4, ENGLAND.

Agents for Indian Railways; Roberts, McLean & Co., Ltd., Calcutta, Bombay and Lahore.

'Phone: Hendon 8045-6.
Cables: Tilley, Hendon.

Agents for South African Railways: The Arban Co., Johannesburg

---

An advertisement for Tilley lamps which provides both illustration and a verbal description which may assist modellers.

An alternative style of post for carrying Tilley lamps (Speen, Lambourn branch).

R. DENISON

column by four short, curved brackets, but others were suspended by their top case from wrought-iron, harp-shaped brackets. There were also wall-mounted lamps. Within the front glass of the lamp there was often a small panel in which the station name was printed, sometimes blue or black letters on clear glass, alternatively, white letters on blue glass.

Yard lamps were not so common at branch stations but where they did occur they were much taller than the platform lamps (perhaps a 14 ft column compared to 8 ft) and were fitted with a larger lamp case, typically of hexagonal rather than square section.

During the Second World War, the black-out saw certain platform and yard lamps adapted with a form of shield which fitted around the top casing. Many of these were not subsequently removed until the line closed, so anyone modelling British Railways Western Region scenes should watch out for these features. They were almost ubiquitous, even on the most strategically unimportant of lines.

Where oil and gas lamps of this format were not provided, the common alternative was the decidedly inferior Tilley lamp. These were carried on tall posts, anything up to 20 ft high. The lamp itself was oil-lit, somewhat akin to a hurricane lamp, which was trimmed at platform level and then hoisted to the top of the post by a wire and pulley. Tilley lamps were widely used on halts and small stations where they probably proved easier to maintain.

Station Fencing and Gates

Two main types of fencing and gates were used at branch stations. The first was manufactured from iron strip and bar. The strip formed the top and bottom rails whilst the bar was used for the upright railings. At a distance the railings appeared round but they were actually of square section, set at an angle of 45 degrees to the top and bottom rails. The upper ends were flattened to provide a 'spear' shape. From inspection of surviving examples, it would seem that standard panels were comprised of two end supports, which were embedded in the ground and braced with diagonal struts which only just showed, and 15 railings. Panels were simply bolted together to form the fence. Gates were manufactured from similar materials to matching designs, usually supported on ornate, cast-iron gateposts.

The other common style was of wooden construction, with vertical,

Standard gas lamp carrying the special wartime shield around the top case. Many of these were not removed subsequently and continued until closure.

A. ATTEWELL

The two common patterns of fencing were the iron 'spear' fencing illustrated at the top of the page and the simple wooden design seen below. Note the triangular section 'arris' rail (sometimes three) used to batten the wooden palings. The spear fence (at Minehead) also sports some rather nice enamelled advertisements.

NATIONAL RAILWAY MUSEUM, A. ATTEWELL and LENS OF SUTTON

A less common dual-height fencing was employed at a number of locations. These illustrations show Coleford (right) and Monmouth Troy (below). A close-up of the same style, again at Monmouth, appears at the head of the page where the top of the main posts have been cut away at an angle. Evidently, such details varied.

D. THOMPSON
G. M. PERKINS
and A. ATTEWELL

Angle-iron arris rails at Faringdon.

A. ATTEWELL

Wooden paling fence with the distinctive 'notched' top. This fence at Cirencester appears to be made entirely of wood but some of these fences were made with angle-iron to batten the palings. An example is seen below, behind the GWR staff member, and on the opposite page, bottom right.
W. A. CAMWELL and CTY. MIKE FENTON

pointed planks, braced by two, sometimes three, longitudinal battens, some 6 in or so from the top and bottom. Panels were made up of 16 vertical planks and were supported on square section wooden posts set in the ground.

The HMRS study *Great Western Way* suggests that these two patterns were the only designs used by the GWR. However, photo evidence shows at least two further styles. Both were constructed with wooden palings but the top of each paling was 'notched' to produce an 'arrow-head', not dissimilar to the metal spear fence. In some cases, triangular section wooden arris rails were used as battens, but close scrutiny of photos reveals some were battened with angle iron. Faringdon had fencing of this type.

A further variation on this design saw palings of half height used alternately. This is illustrated with the example at Monmouth and Coleford (opposite), whilst overleaf Chipping Norton shows the same idea deployed, but with plain rather than notched palings.

Away from the stations proper, Great Western lineside fencing was a relatively simple affair. Wooden, and later concrete, posts were set out along the boundary of the company's property, with galvanised wires stretched between them, the lower

strands being more closely spaced than the upper ones.

Nameboards and Notices

Alongside the station fence one would normally find the station nameboard. Like most of the fixtures I have described, these, too, showed a lot of variation. The style that is most readily recognised had the board carried on two 5 in diameter cast-iron posts, usually about 8 ft high and surmounted with decorative caps. Cast-iron letters, which came in several sizes, were bolted to the board to spell out the name and any supplementary information that was required. However, we should note that first, alternative methods of support were often used, including timber posts of varying designs and discarded rail. At halts, the cast posts were usually substituted with timber alternatives and there were plenty of examples where posts would be absent altogether and boards attached directly to a suitable wall. Secondly, different styles of lettering were used at different periods. The modern style was a simple block lettering without serifs, whereas older styles were more condensed and provided with serifs.

The Great Western also made some use of enamelled station nameboards, probably in the latter part of the 19th century.

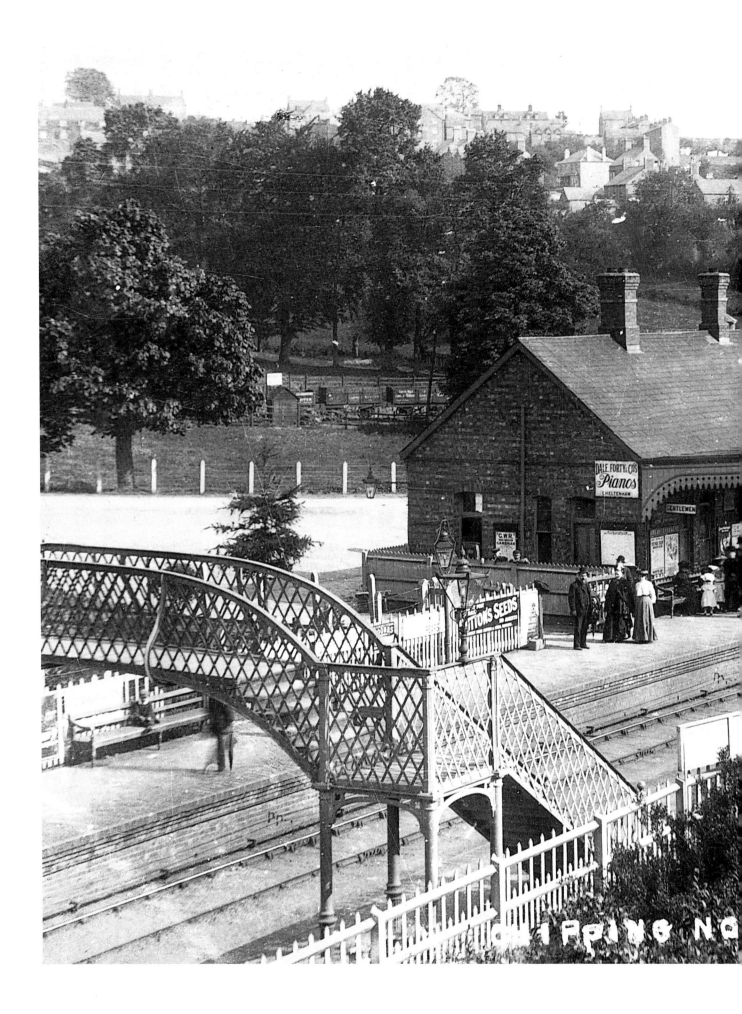

ON STATION.

The independent origins of the Banbury & Cheltenham line are reflected in this pre-World War I photograph of Chipping Norton. The dual-height fencing seen on the previous pages is again used here, albeit in a plain style. The footbridge is not a GWR design but smaller platform equipment, for example the seating, is standard Great Western.
FRANK PACKER

Post and wire fencing of the type that was widely deployed at halts and small stations built or redeveloped in the first decades of the 20th century.
D. THOMPSON and C. GORDON WATFORD

Some were quite long-lived. Portesham on the Abbotsbury branch possessed an example until its removal during the Second World War, as did Tetbury. These boards were blue with white letters whereas the standard board was black.

Stations made extensive use of smaller notices to point directions, identify rooms, prohibit entry to special areas and so forth. These boards were mainly of cast-iron construction. If it were a standard instruction, the whole board would be in one piece but cast letters were available in different sizes to tailor notices to meet specific circumstances. They were normally painted black with white letters although there were variations. Some 19th century photographs show dark letters and a light ground. These may have been blue on white as enamelled signs in this style survived at Tiverton from before the First World War until the mid 1960s. However, this pattern was not adopted on a wide basis.

Two common patterns of station nameboard. The example at Malmesbury employed the older style of lettering whilst at Bromyard the more modern sans-serif style was used. Bromyard also had the standard cast-iron posts to support the board. The advertisement for the Daily Telegraph *suspended beneath the board was a familiar feature at stations all over the system in the 1930s.* JOHN BARNBY and HMRS

Further examples of the variation in station nameboards. Stretton-on-Fosse (top right) shows a 19th century design which did not persist in common usage after 1900. Dymock (top left) appears to be one of the blue enamelled signs. Bourne End (middle left) shows the enlarged board and two sizes of lettering which were often used at junctions. The board at Faringdon (bottom right) was simply painted and may have been new in 1947, when the photograph was taken. Pre-war views do not show a nameboard. NATIONAL RAILWAY MUSEUM, LENS OF SUTTON, A. E. SMITH, JIM BATES, A. ATTEWELL and J. H. RUSSELL

I make no apology for reproducing this well-known official photograph of the new station at Lambourn, since it affords excellent illustration of a range of standard platform and door signs, as well as notice boards and other platform detail.
NATIONAL RAILWAY MUSEUM

Contrasting styles with an early Great Western sign indicating the Ladies' Room and a British Railways enamelled sign for the 'Gents'.
P. J. GARLAND

Standard four-wheeled platform trolleys. Modellers might note the manner in which station staff commonly left trolleys parked in the same area. Detail such as this is important in creating a convincing model.

W. A. CAMWELL
and A. ATTEWELL

For smaller loads, sack trucks were more convenient to manage. Close scrutiny of these photographs suggests that although largely of a similar design, there were detailed differences, particularly in the size and configuration of the luggage 'tray'.

NATIONAL RAILWAY MUSEUM
and A. ATTEWELL

Further illustration of portering equipment. The single-wheeled 'barrow' (centre) was a 19th century design which survived, in small numbers, right through to nationalisation. I am not sufficiently expert on GWR wheelbarrows to state whether the example (bottom) is a standard design or not. But for the modeller, incidental details like this will help to breathe life into our miniature scenes. A. ATTEWELL

PAINTING

To conclude this chapter, I would like to give brief consideration to styles of painting. GWR practice in painting of structures has been thoroughly researched by members of the HMRS and their findings are reported in detail in *Great Western Way*. Extensive repetition here is, therefore, unnecessary. I have summarised the standard practice in *Table 2*, which I hope readers will find useful, but for the detailed account, do look at the HMRS publication.

Colour schemes used by the GWR have been a matter of great debate for many years. In a sense, the passage of time has made such debate increasingly futile since corroborative evidence of colours which have not been seen for the best part of 50 years is not going to emerge now. Even when samples are unearthed from forgotten corners, they can't tell us exactly what the fresh colour looked like since dirt and the fading effects of time must change them. So we must not be too pedantic!

However, we do know that for a large part of the railway's history, two colours, commonly labelled as 'light' and 'dark stone', were the basic shades that were used. Please do not paint your buildings in chocolate and cream. That was a British Railways scheme and was not used by the GWR.

The terms 'light' and 'dark stone' are a little misleading since they suggest these shades were grey or sandy coloured. In practice, there was more than a hint of pink – particularly the 'dark stone' which was a salmon/brown colour – not unlike the shade used by the LSWR in painting the upper panels on its coaches.

This colour was achieved by mixing oxide of iron into a white lead base whilst the 'light' stone had less oxide, or more white, depending upon how you look at it! These colours were actually mixed on the site with colour cards as guides, so there must have been some variation from one station to the next when one allows for different interpretations of the recipe.

There is general agreement on the approximate shade of 'dark stone'. 'Light stone', however, has been the subject of more discussion and I fear that in the process, some questionable ideas have been advanced. Rather surprisingly, one of the sources of uncertainty is the HMRS *Great Western Way*. At the back of this volume is reproduced a colour chart showing all

Table 2.   Basic Patterns of Painting – Structures and Fittings

Structure	Dark Stone	Light Stone	White	Unpainted/ creosote tar
Station buildings (brick/stone)	Door frames and doors, except panels; gutters and downpipes; mouldings on valances and awnings; support columns and ironwork associated with canopies.	Window frames and door panels; bargeboards; woodwork on awnings and valances.	Glazing frames and bars.	
Station buildings (timber)	Main frames, door and window frames, sills; gutters and downpipes; mouldings on valances and awnings; support columns and ironwork associated with canopies.	Door panels; walls, except for framing; bargeboards; woodwork on awnings and valances.	Glazing frames and bars.	
Signal Boxes	Main frames, door frames and doors, except panels; window mullions, sills; bargeboards; gutters and downpipes; steps and rails.	All other woodwork, including door panels.	Glazing bars.	
Goods Sheds (brick/stone)	Door frames, doors except panels; gutters and downpipes; moulding on canopies.	Window frames, door panels bargeboards; woodwork on canopies etc.	Interior walls and roof; glazing frames and bars.	Floors, steps and platforms.
Goods Sheds (timber)	Some had main frames and door frames in this colour.	Some had walls and door panels in this colour.	As above, though some had unpainted glazing frames and bars.	Walls, floors, steps, platforms, some glazing frames and bars.
Engine Sheds	Door frames, doors except panels; gutters and downpipes; roof-light frames.	Window frames, door panels bargeboards; roof supports and smoke extractors.		
Footbridges	Main frames, girders, struts, stair risers; gutters, downpipes; window frames where fitted.	Valances; bargeboards; panels on walk and stairways.	Glazing frames and bars (where fitted).	Steps, floorplank and handrails.
'Pagodas', lamp huts etc.	Window frames and doors; gutters and downpipes.	Walls and sometimes roofs.	Glazing frames and bars.	Some roofs.
Water Towers (conical)	Lower 4 ft of support column in some cases.	All except lower 4 ft of support in some cases.		
Water Towers (rectangular)	Lower 4 ft of support columns edging to main tank, valves etc; door and window frames where present.	All other metalwork, girders and supports; door panels where present.	Glazing frames and bars where present.	
Platform Water Cranes	Lower 4 ft of support column and end of arm.	All other parts.		
Fencing (wood)		All except ironwork on gates which was black.		
Fencing (iron)		All although some photos show black also used.		
Station Nameboard	Support posts and brackets.		Letters, frame (board black).	
Station Seats	All.			
Station Lamps	Lamp housing, base, collar.	All other parts.		
Loading Gauge	Base of Post.	Some may have been this colour.	All other parts.	

Source:– Compiled from notes in the Historical Model Railway Society *Great Western Way*.

the major colours used by the GWR, including the structure colours. 'Light stone' (or Stone No. 2 as it is referred to in this source) is given as a medium grey, almost with a touch of sage about it. This colour was copied, in good faith I'm sure, by at least one manufacturer of paints for modellers. But although this colour chart is said to be derived from official Swindon samples, I don't find this particular shade at all convincing.

My doubt stems from two observations. The first, and more telling, is that in experiments, I have found it impossible to produce the colour by varying quantities of iron oxide and white. You have to add at least one further colour to get the grey element so strongly. But according to instructions (which I have seen) and which are correctly stated in *Great Western Way*, only white lead and iron oxide were used.

It is possible, of course, that old mixes of white lead actually imparted the grey tone but the modern equivalents which I used in my experiments certainly did not.

The second point which strikes me most forcibly about the sample colours given in the HMRS book is that they look *awful* when placed alongside one another! I find it hard to believe that the GWR, which had such a good sense of design, would have allowed two such uncomplementary shades to adorn their buildings for such a long time. My solution, therefore, has been to follow the stated recipe and add more white to the 'dark stone' colour. This provides a lighter pinky/beige tone which I find more convincing. Whether it is correct we will never know, but it does match a surviving example of GWR paint on a well preserved door now at Didcot Railway Centre and the colour prepared

several years ago for Pendon Museum by Compucolor, some tins of which I still possess.

This two-tone pattern of 'stone' colours would be applicable for any date from around 1880 up to nationalisation. In the 1930s, a dark brown was introduced for vulnerable areas such as the bases of timber buildings and sometimes on doors and their frames. With the exception of a small number of signal boxes, I don't see much evidence of this colour within the many hundreds of branch line scenes in the books and photographs in my collection, so I am tempted to suggest that it did not find its way onto too many branches. It is conceivable that branch stations were not repainted as often as busier and more prestigious locations, in which case the diffusion of this colour to secondary routes would be more limited.

Painting of platform valances often employed both standard colours, with the shade being alternated between planks. This is clearly demonstrated in this view of Witney.
LENS OF SUTTON

CHAPTER THREE
TRAFFIC OPERATION

I would like to conclude Part 2 with an examination of branch line traffic and its operation. Whilst models can convey much to the viewer as static scenes, one of the delights of our hobby is the ability to bring the scene to life through the movement of our engines and stock. Furthermore, the significant technical advances in electric control and propulsion

erate quite substantial levels of traffic, the vast majority were not. As we shall see, in passenger workings, two or three coaches were often more than adequate to meet normal needs and in later years, as branches lost passengers to local bus services, the branch engine and its single coach became a very familiar sight. Freight trains, too, were seldom lengthy and in

on branch lines and although some stock was specifically built for branch line work, an awful lot was down-graded from more prestigious workings as it aged and was replaced. Alternatively, vehicles might be transferred from other types of work to branch duties when their capabilities failed to meet changed traffic conditions in their original work areas. Two of the three

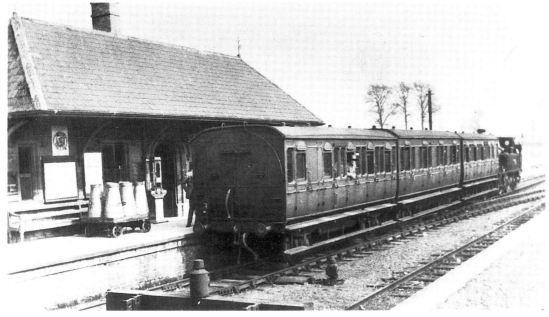

An unidentified 0—4—2T of the '517' class at Faringdon with the branch train. This set of four-wheelers, which included two former Hammersmith & City line coaches, worked the branch for at least forty years.

systems now means that we can make our models perform controlled and complex movements which, in the earlier phases of railway modelling, were not so attainable. Perhaps in consequence, more attention has been focused upon the composition and pattern of working of trains but even so, misunderstanding and uncertainty surrounding real traffic operation is still widespread. So let's see if we can establish at least some of the basic facets of branch operation, Great Western style, in these final pages.

We should start with some general observations on the nature of branch line traffic. Photographs are an excellent source of information on how branch trains were formed and these suggest a number of simple conclusions.

First, we should emphasise the modest scale of most branch trains. Although some lines were sufficiently busy to gen-

some cases, traffic was not so great as to warrant separate goods trains, wagons being tacked onto the rear of the passenger coaches and worked as a mixed train. Working instructions for branch lines normally specified the maximum number of wagons that could be worked in a single train in each direction. At Faringdon, small tank engines were permitted to pull up to 35 wagons marshalled into up trains but in the down direction the number was only 19, owing to adverse gradient in that direction. I would be surprised, though, if these maxima were reached on all but the rarest of occasions and I know that during the mid 1920s, the daily average of wagons moved in and out was only 20 in total, and that divided amongst 9 possible trains.

Secondly, branch trains were a natural repository for older stock. Through time, we see a natural process of evolution in the types of vehicles to be found at work

branch coaches in use at Faringdon during my period of modelling interest were four-wheeled vehicles originally designed by Holden for London suburban services. But when the needs of these services quickly outgrew the rakes of four-wheelers, these little coaches were re-allocated to lesser duties such as rural branch work. Many also ended up in workmen's trains in areas such as the South Wales coalfield.

Thirdly, with a few exceptions, there was relatively little specialised traffic to be seen on branches. Modellers are often lured by the creative offerings of manufacturers into stocking their layouts with interesting and unusual vehicles though sadly, few of these are genuinely relevant to authentic branch line working. By all means support our manufacturers and make models that interest and satisfy you – I do all the time. But make sure you have a decent stock of 'basic' vehicles too, so that when the occasion demands, we can show traffic that was representative of real branches.

I think these general remarks will be reinforced if we now move on to consider stock allocation to branch line duties, starting with locomotives.

LOCOMOTIVE ALLOCATIONS

Readers who really wish to explore this subject in detail will find that lists of engine allocations can be consulted at the PRO at Kew. However, you may find it more convenient to be guided by the two very useful summaries compiled by Ian Harrison and Nigel Pocock for 1921 and 1934 or even better, perhaps, by the visual evidence of photographs of the period in which you are interested.

As a generalisation, at least, we can see the allocation of locomotives to branch lines as being a product of three elements; the physical capacity of the line as reflected in its route classification code, the traffic requirements and the availability of engines.

The ability of a branch line to take different engines was determined by the constraints of track conditions (tight curves or short run-round areas, for example) and particularly, the specified levels of loading for civil engineering structures such as bridges. At Faringdon, medium and large tender engines were prohibited partly by their weight but especially because with only some 49 ft between the engine release points and the platform stop blocks, it was impossible for all but the smallest engines to run round a train in the normal fashion.

The GWR measured the loading as the maximum weight transferred through any one driving axle, and engines and routes were colour-coded according to this loading factor. The lightest category were the 'uncoloured' engines which were less than 14 tons per axle, followed in increasing weight by yellow, blue, red and double red. The only double red engines were the 'King' class which weighed in at 22 tons 10 cwt per axle. Most branches were in the yellow (up to 16 tons) and uncoloured categories, though blue routes (up to 17 tons 12 cwt) and even red routes (over 17 tons 12 cwt but excluding 'Kings') could be found. Working instructions for the different branches usually specified which types of engine were

Early views of branch lines are not always easy to come by; this picture of Presteign station in September 1875 features a '302' class 0−6−0 saddle tank.   COLLECTION MIKE LLOYD

acceptable although this did not mean that those types necessarily appeared.

The fact that the majority of branches were in the lower categories of route classification tended to mean that branch engines would naturally be towards the small and light end of the range. However, in most cases this would be reinforced by the traffic needs of the branch. Most branch trains were short, reflecting the modest levels of demand for the service and in these circumstances, the armies of small tank engines that we associate with branch operations, were ideal for the job.

Allocations would also be conditioned by the availability of engines. Some branches were served for years by the same engine. No. 1473 *Fair Rosamund*, for example, worked the Woodstock branch for most of the period between 1890 and 1935. But when the branch engine was away for repairs or just a washout, its replacement might be whatever was to hand and suitable for the work. So from time to time, all kinds of engine could occur on branches and whilst some lines showed a monotonous uniformity of engines, others reveal surprising variety.

Details on the use of engines in the early periods of branch operation are rather shrouded in the mists of time. Accurate information on broad gauge periods, whether documentary or photographic, is very fragmentary and it is not really until

the late 1890s that we start to see a really clear picture of the types of engines to be seen on branches. The few broad gauge photos of which I am aware, covering branches such as Abingdon, Brixham and Falmouth, mostly show small 2−4−0, 4−4−0 and 0−6−0 saddle tanks. These include Great Western engines of the 'Leo' class but also engines of the South Devon Railway, often quite a long way from their original home.

In the last quarter of the 19th century, the Great Western introduced a large number of small, standard gauge engines for a variety of lighter duties. Many were particularly long-lived and continued to work branches until after the First World War and in exceptional cases, the Second World War.

There is a temptation to view the 0−6−0 tank engines as being similar to the point of uniformity. Closer scrutiny will reveal, however, delightful variation amongst these older designs. Saddle tanks, panniers, side tanks, outside frames, inside frames – they were all there in all kinds of combinations and with lots of detailed variations. Some were ex-broad gauge engines converted to the standard gauge, most were new designs introduced to meet the expanding traffic of the 1880s and 1890s.

Branch line modellers interested in the period from the 1890s up to the mid-1920s, should pay particular attention to three saddle tank classes which were widely used on local services. The '1076' or 'Buffalo' class was a sturdy 0–6–0 whilst the '850' and '2021' classes, also 0–6–0s, were smaller-wheeled cousins. The '1076' class were outside-framed whilst the '850' and '2021' were inside-framed, but all were very long-lived designs, despite their old-fashioned appearance. Later in their lives many of these engines, particularly the '2021' and '1076' classes, were modified by the substitution of pannier tanks, and, later still, some received full rather than half cabs. In this form they began to resemble more modern pannier engines but this illusion would only be momentary as the outside frames and the springs on the footplate of the 'Buffalo' or the small wheels of the '2021' would soon betray their antiquity.

What appears to be one of the '1076' ('Buffalo') class of 0–6–0 tanks, photographed at Carbis Bay on its way to St. Ives. This engine is in its original condition. Many were rebuilt with panniers and new cabs. LENS OF SUTTON

Another common branch engine, a '2021' class 0–6–0 tank, at Bridport around the turn of the century. LENS OF SUTTON

A '645' class 0–6–0 tank No. 1552, photographed on the New Radnor line. These engines were outwardly similar to the '2021' class, but had larger driving wheels and a higher footplate which helped to make them distinct. LENS OF SUTTON

An '850' class engine at Cardigan. Comparison with the picture on the previous page shows how these engines were a smaller version of the '2021' class.
LENS OF SUTTON

Rebuilding often disguised the origin of these 0–6–0 tanks. No. 2001 was actually a member of the '850' classs, but new tanks, boiler fittings and bunker produced an engine with few traces of the original design.
LENS OF SUTTON

No. 2080 belonged to the '2021' class and provides another comparison with the smaller '850s'.
COLLECTION P. KARAU

Further variations are reflected in these illustrations. No. 1256 was a 'Buffalo' class engine, shown here after rebuilding. No. 1888 (centre) belonged to the '1854' class whilst No. 2795 (bottom) was from the '2721' class. All were originally saddle tanks.

AUTHOR'S COLLECTION

A '655' class 0–6–0 tank, No. 1742, shunting at Fair-ford in 1947, over fifty years after it first entered service. J. H. RUSSELL

Two examples of the larger modern 0–6–0 pannier tanks introduced after World War I. The '54XX' class (left) were intro-duced in 1930. With their 5ft 2in wheels, these were fast little engines and initial duties often saw them working stopping trains along main lines. They led to the '64XX' class and '74XX' class (above), the latter intro-duced in 1936. The '64XX' and '74XX' had the 4ft 7½in driving wheels that were usual for 0–6–0 tanks. The '64XXs' were auto-fitted whilst the '74XXs' worked at a higher boiler pressure and were more powerful engines.
R. K. BLENCOWE
and L. B. LAPPER

Contemporary with these engines was a very important branch engine, the 0–4–2T '517' class. These were built in large numbers over a period of some 20 years from 1868 and lists of engine allocations show that they formed the mainstay of services on a large number of branches in all parts of the system. The class can be a difficult one to model because the length of time over which they were built ensured there was considerable detailed variation. These differences were then further compounded by selective modernisation, for example through the replacement of round-topped fireboxes with Belpaire designs on many members of the class, but not all. Most lost the tall, elegant chimneys that adorned the class before 1910. The advice here, therefore, is try to find a photograph of the particular

The '517' class 0–4–2 tank was a very common branch engine although for modellers the class poses problems because of the numerous detailed variations between members. These variations included wheel spacing, boiler fittings, firebox design, cab and bunker design and trailing wheel bearings. Some of these points are reflected in these illustrations. No. 534 (top) has a round-topped firebox and outside bearings on the trailing wheel whilst No. 835 (bottom) has the Belpaire firebox and inside bearings. The '3571' class possessed an extended footplate valance which incorporated the cab steps and the trailing axle bearings. This is illustrated on No. 3580 (centre) which also shows the rear spectacle plate with which some of these and the '517' class were originally fitted.
J. J. KITE and PHOTOMATIC

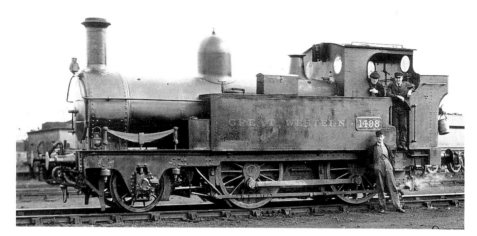

engine you are modelling, in the correct period.

A significant number of branches were allocated the 2–4–0 'Metro' tanks. Their original use was for fast local passenger trains and some were fitted with condensing apparatus for working the underground routes in London. But with more than 130 engines placed in service, it was inevitable that some would find their way, if only by chance, onto branches, whilst others were clearly allocated to such duties as a matter of policy. Faringdon was occasionally visited by a 'Metro' and the locomotive allocations for 1921 mentioned earlier, show these engines at Cirencester, Fairford, Henley, Marlow and Minehead, amongst others.

Branch workings never drew much of a distinction between passenger and freight duties so the special freight engines were not necessarily a part of the branch scene, except within South Wales. However, we cannot leave the 19th century without passing reference to the 'Dean Goods' 0–6–0 tender engine and its less well-known predecessors, like the 'Armstrong Goods'. With their light axle loading, these engines could go virtually anywhere and, although as tender engines they were not ideally suited to branch work, many were so used.

The 'Metro' class of 2–4–0 tank was also subject to variation, although not to the extent of the '517' class. The principal distinction was between the so-called 'large' and 'small' Metros. The 'large Metros' had side tanks extended forward to a point just behind the leading axle box; the 'small Metros' had tanks which were noticeably shorter. This affected the front axle springing so that on the 'large Metro', the laminated springs were replaced by a more compact group of volute springs. Comparison of 'large Metro' No. 3585 (bottom) with the two 'small Metros' (above) reveals these differences, as well as contrasting styles of cab and bunker. COLLECTION P. KARAU, H. C. CASSERLEY and J. H. RUSSELL

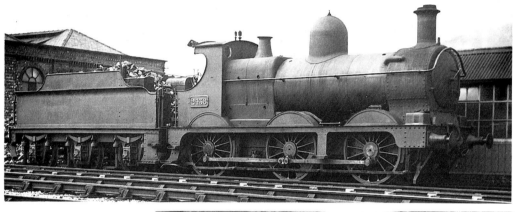

The 'Dean Goods' was a classic design — a versatile engine which could work fast passenger trains just as readily as the freight workings for which it was initially intended. The top view shows No. 2323 with a southbound passenger train on the MSWJR at Marlborough. The old GWR terminus features in the background on the far side of the boundary fence. Above: No. 2438 c.1938/9. Below: A really evocative scene of a Dean Goods at work in Bar End yard at Winchester on the Didcot, Newbury & Southampton Railway.

J. E. KITE
W. VAUGHAN JENKINS
and COLLECTION
I. D. BEALE

Some branch line 'oddities'. Top: *Ex-South Devon Railway 2–4–0T (GWR No. 1300) taking water at Hemyock in 1929.* Centre: *GWR 4–4–0T No. 13 pictured at Looe.* Above: *Ex-Monmouthshire Railway & Canal Co. 4–4–0T (GWR No. 1306) at Radley on a train of four-wheeled coaches for Abingdon.* H. C. CASSERLEY and L & GRP, CTY. DAVID & CHARLES

It is also worth mentioning the occasional 'oddities' which worked some branches. The 4–4–0 saddle tank, No. 13, which worked the Looe branch or the 0–4–4 side tank engines, Nos. 34 and 35, which worked the awkward St. Ives and Helston lines, come immediately to mind. So does the little ex-South Devon Railway 2–4–0 tank which features in H. C. Casserley's famous views of Hemyock. The ex-Monmouthshire Railway & Canal Co. 4–4–0T, No. 1306, worked the Abingdon and Abbotsbury branches at various stages of its career before withdrawal in the early years of the 20th century.

Thanks to the generosity of my friend John Copsey, I am able to provide illustration of the allocations of a cross-section of these early engines, in this instance for 1906 (*Table 3*). This is not meant to represent an exhaustive list but seeks to

Table 3.   Allocations of Engines to Branches – 1906

Engine Class	Allocations
'2021'	Lydney, Cirencester, Kington, Easton, Watlington, Bridport.
'517'	Abingdon, Ashburton, Brixham, Faringdon, Blagdon, Marlborough, Corwen, Yatton, Wells, Cirencester, Hooton, Alcester, Chard, Moretonhampstead, Tetbury, Lambourn, Woodstock.
'Metro'	Watlington, Marlow, Henley on Thames, Newquay, Fairford, Kingsbridge, Ashburton, Staines, Brixham, Moretonhampstead, Minehead, Bala, Blaenau Ffestiniog.
'633'	Staines, Pencader, Tenby.
'645'	Newcastle Emlyn, Corwen, Tenby, Pencader.
'1501'	Bala, Corwen, Trawsfynydd, Much Wenlock.
'1076'	Faringdon, Cirencester, Calne, Tenby, Newquay, Wells, Pembroke Dock, Chard, Moretonhampstead.
'850'	Newquay, Wallingford, Cardigan, Shipston-on-Stour, Bodmin, St. Ives, Lambourn.
'1016'	Calne, Launceston, Pembroke Dock.
'3201'	Winchester (for DN & S), Falmouth, Tenby, Wells.
'2301'	Pencader, Winchester.
'3521'	Didcot (for DN & S), Falmouth, Launceston.

provide indication of the relative importance of different classes whilst also drawing attention to some of the rarer types that were a part of the pre-1914 branch line scene.

At the turn of the century, the replacement of William Dean by G. J. Churchward saw a revolution in engine and carriage design. At first, lowly branch lines were immune from many of the changes but Churchward's standardised approach was nothing if it was not comprehensive, and new designs for small branch engines duly began to replace some of the veteran engines of the 19th century.

Churchward particularly favoured the 2–6–2 'Prairie' tank and several variants, the 44XX, 45XX and 55XX were especially designed with branch and secondary workings in mind. Their light axle load, combined with additional power derived from the larger engine, made them especially suitable for improving branch services.

However, we need to be careful in making selections for a model railway since these new engines did not find equal use in all parts of the system. Their attributes were best utilised on the steeply graded and/or busy West Country

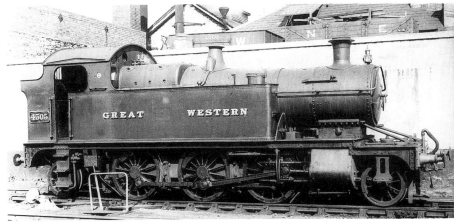

Three of Churchward's Prairie tank engines. Top: *No. 4578 at Gloucester.* Centre: *No. 4505.* Above: *No. 4403 outside the shed at Much Wenlock. The '4400' class were the smallest of the Prairie tanks and were designed particularly for the hilly West Country branches. No. 4578 belonged to the '4575' class, a development of the '4500' engines but with larger tanks to extend their range.*
HMRS, COLLECTION ALAN HALL and W. A. CAMWELL

The '48XX' class 0–4–2 tanks were introduced in 1932, primarily as replacements for the elderly '517' class engines. Accordingly, these became important branch line engines for the latter period of the GWR and throughout steam operation on British Railways. Many, including No. 4868, were fitted for working auto coaches.
LENS OF SUTTON

branches, and locomotive allocations show these engines being used first at locations such as Helston, Kingsbridge, Launceston, Moretonhampstead, Princetown and St. Ives. Elsewhere, the Victorian engines persisted and although I have indulged myself in building one of Malcolm Mitchell's superb kits for the 45XX 'Small Prairie', it is quite inappropriate for Faringdon as, to the best of my knowledge, none were ever seen on the line.

Churchward also produced a larger version of these 'Prairies', the 31XX class, but their axle loading excluded them from many branch lines and they were most at home on fast suburban services in the London, Birmingham and Bristol divisions. We don't really find them working branch lines until British Railways days,

The modernised versions of the elderly 0–6–0 tanks reviewed earlier included the very successful '57XX' class of pannier engines. This unidentified member of the class is shown at Blackmill on the line from Bridgend to Nantymoel and Gilfach Goch in South Wales.
W. A. CAMWELL

Ex-MSWJ 4–4–0 No. 8, rebuilt by the GWR and running as No. 1126, is shown on its home territory at Marlborough. J. E. KITE

so Great Western modellers should be wary of how they use these engines.

When Collett replaced Churchward in 1922 new engines duly followed. Collett was a master at taking a good design and improving it. Thus Dean's '517' class became the well-loved 14XX and 48XX engines; the new 57XX 0–6–0 pannier tanks provided a more powerful development of the smaller engines discussed earlier, whilst new designs such as the '2251' 0–6–0 tender engine also appeared. When first introduced, the 57XX and '2251' were not really intended for branch work and it was only in the later stages of their careers that they found their way into such duties, although by the mid-1930s, the '2251s' were at work on cross-country lines such as the Didcot and Newbury and the old Midland and South Western route.

Mention of the M & SWJR reminds that we should not overlook the absorbed engines. After the Grouping in 1923, the GWR inherited a very large number of engines formerly owned by the independent companies. The fate of these locomotives varied. Some were promptly sold or scrapped, others continued as before, but most were eventually rebuilt by the GWR at Swindon. After rebuilding they could be allocated anywhere but they tended to be returned to former territories.

A lovely photograph of '2251' class No. 2226 heading south on the Didcot & Newbury line near Burghclere. J. F. RUSSELL-SMITH

So branches in South Wales, for example, were extensively worked by rebuilt engines on the Taff Vale, Rhymney, Barry and Brecon & Merthyr Railways and their lesser counterparts, alongside standard GWR engines. For modellers these are awkward subjects as most are scratch-building projects. On the positive side, though, absorbed engines are quite well documented and provide a change from usual GWR motive power. For a South Wales scene, they are essential.

Before we leave consideration of the types of engines associated with branch lines, we must acknowledge the role of the steam railmotors. This was another of Churchward's innovations for the GWR, the first railmotors being introduced in 1903. At that stage there was doubtless high expectation that they would provide a cheap and convenient vehicle for operating local services along main lines and branches. Their limitations, particularly their inability to pull additional vehicles when their own accommodation was filled, were only realised gradually, and separate or extra engines would still be needed for regular goods workings. Ordinary engines fitted to work autotrains quickly proved more useful and adaptable, and the working life of most railmotors was relatively short. Although some lasted into the 1930s, others went as early as 1914 and many were converted to auto trailers in the 1920s.

To see where they were used, we must delve into the period around the First World War. I have been fortunate to consult a copy of the complete Working Programmes for July 1911 and this details widespread use of railmotors on branches. In the west, St. Ives, Helston, Newquay, Perranporth, Yealmpton, Clevedon and Abbotsbury were all being served by these vehicles. In South Wales, services such as Lampeter to Aberystwyth, Tenby to Pembroke Dock, Newport to Merthyr and Monmouth to Ross were worked by railmotors, whilst in the north, Oswestry, Corwen and Llangollen also had them. So they were clearly used in many parts of the system, although restricted in period.

The preceding text has attempted to illustrate the range of engines that were a part of the traditional Great Western branch scene, together with something of their chronology. Over time there was a reasonably predictable process of evolution in locomotive allocations to branches, and as modellers we might choose to take a broad time span to illustrate that process

or focus upon a narrower time period which featured engines and stock that are particularly to our taste. Let's close this section with another example to illustrate a sequence of engine allocations through time. In his book on the Yealmpton branch, A. R. Kingdom provides such a list from 1900 up to the period of the Second World War. In the 1900s, passenger trains were being worked by railmotors and double-framed 0–6–0 saddle tanks of the '1501' class, whilst freight was handled by 'Dean Goods' engines and

An auto train with the engine (probably a '517' class tank) propelling the coach, at Bloxham on the Banbury & Cheltenham line.   FRANK PACKER

2–6–0 'Aberdares' – something of a rarity on branches outside South Wales. (These latter two may have been special war-time allocations.) By the 1920s the pattern had changed, with most services being worked by 0–6–0 pannier tanks of the '1076' class with auto coaches on passenger trains, supplemented with steam railmotors (which worked up to 1929). In the 1940s, when the line was again being worked after a period in which traffic had been suspended, 'Small Prairies' of the 44XX class were in service with 0–6–0 panniers

Steam railmotor No. 97 at Ashton on the Teign Valley branch on 24th July 1930.   F. M. GATES

A Plymouth train accelerating away from Yelverton. The engine, a 'small Metro' 2–4–0 tank, is pulling a lovely mixture of coaches painted in the pre-1908 livery. All are non-corridor stock with, at the head of the train, a van third (Dia. D24) followed by a six-wheeled luggage composite (probably Dia. U16). Behind the six-wheel coach comes one of the numerous eight-compartment thirds, and at the tail, another luggage composite, one of the short bogie coaches built in the early 1880s, possibly to Dia. E10 or E13. The start of the branch to Princetown features in the background.
LENS OF SUTTON

of the 54XX and 37XX classes. Quite a range and, with the exception of the 'Aberdare', fairly characteristic.

COACHING STOCK

The development of passenger services on branches followed a pattern that was every bit as interesting and varied as the allocation of engines. During the last quarter of the 19th century (which is the earliest period for which I have documentary and photographic records), branch passenger trains were mainly composed of short wheelbase four- and six-wheeled stock. These began to be supplemented, towards the turn of the century, by eight-wheeled bogie coaches, although the smaller four-wheelers remained at work on many branches until at least the 1930s.

The availability of a popular set of 4 mm scale plastic kits for Great Western four-wheeled coaches has rather encouraged a view amongst modellers that these particular designs are entirely representative. This understandable, though not necessarily accurate perception, has closed some modellers' eyes to the fact that there were dozens of different patterns for four- and six-wheelers, many being far more

numerous than the particular style depicted in the kit.

The lack of appropriate variety in the modelling of late Victorian short stock is partly a reflection of the limited offering of such coaches from the trade (although at least three manufacturers of etched brass kits have four- and six-wheeled coaches in

their lists) but more particularly, I think, is a product of the relative dearth of authoritative information on the subject within what I would call the 'accessible' literature.

This is unfortunate because photographs of branch trains of the late 19th century often reveal lovely blends of stock. The GWR developed a reputation for

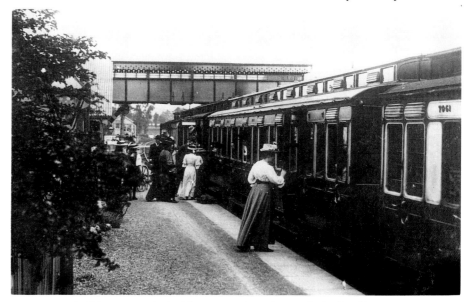

Martock in the Edwardian period, with passengers boarding a train for Yeovil.
LENS OF SUTTON

Bugle station on the Newquay branch in Cornwall. The 2−4−0 'small Metro' tank is pulling a characteristically mixed train; a six-wheeled, centre luggage composite is followed by one of the 50ft non-clerestory brake composites (Dia. E40), another six-wheeled composite and a passenger brake van. The leading vehicle may well be one of the coaches originally built for the broad gauge and converted after 1892.

L & GRP, CTY. DAVID & CHARLES

An unidentified 'Metro' class 2−4−0T with the Moretonhampstead branch train c.1900.   COLLECTION J. E. KITE

A busy scene at Bromyard c.1905. The double-headed train and the activity on the station forecourt suggest some sort of 'special'.

never marshalling two coaches of the same style into the same train and that is certainly borne out by visual evidence.o Mixing of clerestory and non-clerestory coaches was quite common and it was not unusual to find an eight-wheeled coach trapped in the middle of a train of four- and six-wheelers. There were also four-wheeled passenger brake vans which used to 'top and tail' trains and helped contribute to the medley.

Contemporary with the development of the fleets of four- and six-wheelers, William Dean introduced bogie clerestory stock for main line work. Many of these vehicles, particularly the 48 ft stock, were non-corridor and when, in the 1890s, longer corridor coaches became more widely available, the earlier vehicles began to find their way onto secondary and branch line duties.

Construction of four- and six-wheeled coaches for branch lines continued up to 1902 but then Churchward took over and things changed quite radically. We have already seen how Churchward's immediate response to traffic needs of branch and local workings was the introduction of the railmotor. However, the railmotor fleet was complemented by the simultaneous introduction of auto-trailers, perhaps the

The Tetbury branch train c.1907.

COLLECTION R. S. CARPENTER

most familiar of all Great Western branch line coaches.

The auto-coach was, of course, ideal for branch line working and from their introduction in the years before the First World War, they were widely employed on secondary duties until after the demise of the GWR. In truth they are a study in

themselves and I do urge readers to consult the specialist coaching sources. There were many different designs which spanned a period of building up to 1954. The biggest were a magnificent 70 ft length but most were shorter (between 57 ft and 60 ft). Earliest designs were wooden with moulded panels although later styles were

A '4575' Prairie tank leaving Falmouth with a local service to Truro in the 1920s. The rear three vehicles probably formed one of the branch 'sets' at the time, since they appear in other photographs. The leading clerestory might be a strengthening vehicle to cater for some additional traffic. The leading and trailing coaches in the set are both 50ft composites to Diagram E40 and date from 1895. COLLECTION R. S. CARPENTER

Perhaps the classic Great Western branch train, though far from universal. An auto-coach and engine waiting to depart Blenheim & Woodstock with a service to Kidlington, or maybe Oxford. The coach is one of the 70ft trailers built to Diagram L between 1905 and 1908. Most lasted into BR ownership. J. H. MOSS

Over the years, the Lambourn branch saw some delightful combinations of coaches in its trains. Here '850' class 0—6—0 saddle tank No. 2007 is heading a train with one of the many eight-compartment clerestory thirds from the 1890s and an auto trailer, here used as an ordinary service coach. The trailer is one of the 70ft Diagram L series, possibly No. 58, which was used regularly on this branch. The third vehicle, largely obscured by steam, is a clerestory van third.
LENS OF SUTTON

plainer and made of steel. Some were conversions of railmotors. Inevitably, over long working lives, many auto coaches were subject to modification. Bogies might be changed, panels or ventilators sheeted over, buffers replaced etc. It pays the modelmaker, therefore, to look very carefully at chosen prototypes, partly to get the model right, partly also in the hope of finding something out of the ordinary. The auto-trailer is such a cliché for Great Western modellers that models which demonstrate the range and variation in a design which the uninitiated assume to be uniform, will always be welcome.

In pursuing this line, this is perhaps another juncture at which to sound a note of caution. There is a great temptation to equate autotrains with branch line workings. Many branches were worked by auto-coaches but it is not true of all. Far from it in fact. Coach Working Programmes show extensive use of sets of standard coaches for branch and local duties and there were lines where I am quite sure auto-coaches were never used.

The auto-coaches were the only designs of Churchward's period that were clearly

Corridor stock was not common on branches but was used on some of the longer cross-country routes. The location of this photograph is not known, but the use of a 'Duke' class engine and the two-coach train suggests either the Didcot—Southampton line, or perhaps the old M & SWJR.
H. E. S. SIMMONS

Wells (Tucker Street) with a pair of B-sets standing at the platforms on 21st April 1934. Note how on these semi-permanent formations the traffic division and set number were marked on the ends of the coaches.
                                                                                                    H. C. CASSERLEY

intended for branch work. As we will see a little later, 'Toplights' and other main line coaches would have been seen on some lines as through coaches. But apart from suburban sets which worked some branches in the London, Birmingham and Bristol divisions, most of the new designs at this time were not intended for branches.

Soon after Collett took over, another favourite coach with branch line modellers appeared. Amongst the new steel-panelled non-corridor stock introduced between 1924 and 1929 was a close-coupled brake composite which, when linked to another of identical style, created the B-set. It should, I think, be emphasised that the B-set was simply a standard formation (see

later), and, over the next decade or so, several different styles of coach were manufactured for use as B-sets. (The first batches of B-sets utilised vehicles built to Diagram E129 whilst later versions employed Dias. E140, E145 and E147.) However, like the auto-coach, the B-set has become an accepted (and expected) part of the Great Western scene from the 1920s onwards. But like the auto-coach, the same proviso over the use of B-sets applies. Many branches did see this style of working, although it was far from universal.

By the 1930s, many rural branch lines were already firmly fixed on the downward path towards eventual closure, particularly as road transport began to become established and competitive. Thus, apart from the batches of replacement auto-trailers mentioned earlier, there was little significant construction of new vehicles for branch services after this time. Instead, branch lines again became the recipients of main line coaches which had been downgraded. Reduction in passenger levels also meant that now one coach would often suffice where in the past two or three might have been necessary.

For single coach branch working in later years, two types of vehicle were com-

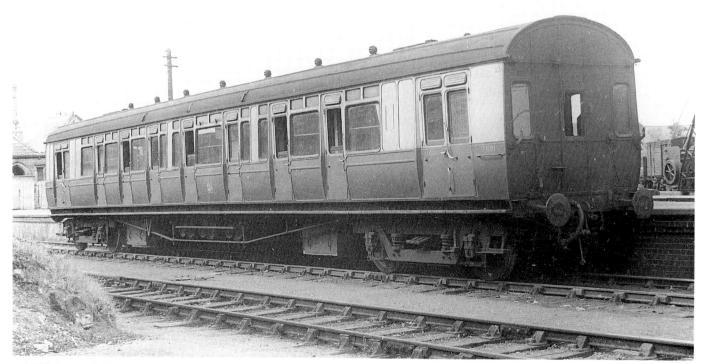

A 70ft 'concertina' slip coach (with slipping gear removed) at Faringdon in 1947. A number of branches received these coaches in their latter days, the single vehicle often being all that traffic conditions demanded.
                                                                                                    P. J. GARLAND

monly used. The first was the standard brake composite which, by definition, afforded first and third class accommodation, luggage space and a guard's compartment, i.e. all that would normally be required to run a service. Wooden-bodied 'Toplights' from before the First World War or early steel-panelled vehicles from the 1920s were frequently used in this way.

An alternative was to use ex-slip coaches, with the slipping gear removed. Although slip coach working continued on British Railways Western Region until 1960, the gradual contraction in slip workings during the 1930s and '40s released older slip coaches for other duties. As a 'self-contained' vehicle they were ideal for working short branch lines, which is where many ended their days. Branches served by 'Toplight' and/or 'Concertina' ex-slip coaches included Lambourn, Henley, Newcastle Emlyn and Faringdon.

I have tried to indicate the main types of coaches that provided the basis for branch operations at different phases of the company's history but we should also give some attention to how they were composed into trains. Train formations were carefully set out in the various programmes of Coach Workings. Great Western trains also ran in a variety of set formations, many of which are not familiar to modellers.

Let us start with *Table 4*. I have compiled this from a rare, complete set of Coach Working Programmes for July 1911 and it seeks to summarise the train formations in use on a comprehensive cross-section of branch lines. I presume these to be the sets which were kept on the lines in question, as distinct from other sets which may have ventured down some of these branches as part of a more elaborate working (see later).

Several observations are worth making. First, and most striking, is the widespread use of four- and six-wheeled stock in these branch formations. (The absence of any description in the 'Notes' section of the table might be taken to imply 8-wheeled vehicles were in use on these routes, although this is not certain.) Although we are here into the second decade of the 20th century (just!), the small stock still dominates branch services. Auto-trains were not, apparently, widespread, though separate listings show them as working the Lambourn and Abbotsbury branches.

A second feature is the number of lines where the branch train is made up of two

Table 4. Branch and Local Train Formations – July 1911

Division/Line	Van	First	Third	Brake Compo	Compo	Brake Third	Notes
London Division							
Uxbridge			1		2	2	
Staines			1	2	2		
Marlow	1		1		2	1	6-wheel stock
Henley					2	2	6-wheel stock / 8-wheel stock
Wallingford					1	2	4-wheel stock
Abingdon					1	2	4-wheel stock
Faringdon					1	2	4-wheel stock
Marlborough					2		8-wheel stock
Blenheim					2		8-wheel stock
Fairford	1	1	2		2	1	6-wheel stock
Bristol Division							
Highworth					1	2	4-wheel stock
Malmesbury					1	2	4-wheel stock
Bridport			1		1	2	4-wheel stock
Blagdon					1	2	4-wheel stock
Avonmouth			2		1	2	
Exeter Division							
Chard					2	2	
Exe Valley					2	2	
Tiverton					1	2	
Culm Valley			1				
Brixham					1	2	
Plymouth Division							
Ashburton					1	2	
Kingsbridge			1		1	2	
Princetown			1	2			
Yealmpton							Railmotor
Looe			1		1	2	
Wadebridge					2	1	
Bodmin					2	1	
Helston			2				
St. Ives		1	2				
Perranporth							Railmotor
Gloucester Division							
Cirencester	1			2			
Tetbury			1			1	4-wheel stock
Presteign					1	1	4-wheel stock
Pontypool Road Division							
Dowlais	1		1		1	1	
Coleford				1			
Golden Valley					1	2	4-wheel stock
Cardiff Division							
Ely Valley	1		2		1	1	6-wheel stock
Nantymoel			2		1	2	8-wheel stock
Blaengarw			2		1	2	8-wheel stock
Abergwnfi			1		1	2	8-wheel stock
Porthcawl			1		1	2	8-wheel stock
Swansea Division							
Llandyssul	1		2		2	1	4/6-wheel st.
Milford Haven				2		1	
Cardigan	1		1		2	1	4-wheel stock
Newcastle Emlyn	1		1		2		6-wheel stock
Worcester Division							
Alcester	1		1				van 4 wheels
Much Wenlock					1	2	
Shipston on Stour			1				
Northern Division							
Blaenau Ffest'og		1	1		1	2	3 sets of 4-wheeled stock
		1	1		1	2	
Oswestry			1		1	2	

4–4–0 'Duke' class engine No. 3255 Excalibur *leaving Didcot for Newbury, via the DN & S line. The presence of racing stables on the Berkshire Downs ensured that horse-box traffic was always quite prominent on the Newbury line. Behind the horse-boxes are a collection of late 19th century coaches, including a composite and a 40ft passenger brake van.*   J. E. KITE

Brake Thirds (or Van Thirds in GWR parlance) together with a Composite which normally would be rostered between the two Third class vehicles. This might almost be considered a standard formation for branch work at this time. Faringdon appears to have been worked continuously by such a combination for about 40 years! However, the table also reveals a lot of variation ranging from the extremes of single coach working on the Culm Valley, Alcester and Shipston lines to a rake of seven vehicles on the Fairford branch.

The Fairford line train was unusual in containing a First class coach. In practice, such accommodation on branch trains was always very limited so that in a typical three-coach set with a Composite and two Van Thirds, just two compartments might be available for First class passengers. Even this meagre allocation must have been unused on many journeys. The minor role of First class coaches in branch work is perhaps emphasised by the disappearance of the vehicle mentioned in the Fairford train by July 1922. Then the formation was given as 2 Vans, 2 Thirds, and 2 Compos, although still six-wheeled stock.

Quite a number of the formations given for 1911 were still in use in 1922, for example at Brixham, Culm Valley and Tiverton in the Exeter Division; at Marlow and Wallingford in the London Division, and at Highworth and Faringdon in the Bristol Division. (Faringdon was transferred from London to Bristol Division sometime between 1911 and

1922.) However, other branches show revised formations, often with additional vehicles providing strengthening. In scouring the Coach Working Programmes, some lovely trains come to light. In the Swansea Division for 1922, the Newcastle Emlyn branch is given as being worked by a set of 6-wheeled coaches (Compo-Van-Third) coupled to two 8-wheeled coaches (Van Third-Compo). In the London Division at the same time, the Watlington and Lambourn

lines were each worked by a 60 ft trailer and a 6-wheeled Van Third.

With the passage of time, these fascinating combinations tend to be replaced by more uniform standard formations. There were exceptions as some of the lesser branches retained 4-wheeled coaches into the 1930s and strange combinations could never be ruled out. One of my favourite pictures of unusual branch trains was taken by S. W. Baker on the Lambourn line and shows diesel railcar No. 18 hauling a Van

Table 5.   Examples of Standard Coach Formations

Year	Set Formations				
1911	A	B	C		
	Van Third Third Compo Van Third	Van Third Compo Compo Third Van	Van Third Compo Compo Third Third Third Van Third		
1922	M (6-wheel)	WW (4-wheel)			
	Van Third Compo Compo Third Van	Van Third Third Compo Van Third			
1930	A	B	D	M	W
	Van Third Third First Third Van Third	Bk Compo Bk Compo	Van Third Compo Compo Van Third	Van Third Third Lav Compo Van Third	Bk Compo Third Third Third Third Third Third Bk Compo

Third clerestory and a covered goods wagon. Great stuff!

I am uncertain when the GWR began to identify standard formations. The 1911 document is inconsistent in that some divisions give standard formations whilst others appear not to. The usual practice where it was used, was to identify the different sets with a letter which thus saved

time and space in describing trains in Working Programmes. However, the same prefix letter did not necessarily have a consistent meaning across all the divisions.

We have already touched upon the B-set but there were many others. Unfortunately, their designation and composition is not consistent through time so that although by the mid-1920s the B-set was the familiar combination of two Brake Composites, in 1911 it was a six-coach set (Van-Third-Compo-Compo-Third-Van).

I won't discuss all the formations, that would become tedious. Instead I have set out some examples in *Table 5*, together with dates when these formations were in use. But it is worth highlighting some of the formations that might be of particular interest to branch line modellers.

In the 1922 workings, for instance, we find the M- and WW-sets. These little trains make a very suitable subject for branch and local services. The M-sets could be used as stopping trains along main lines but might also take in branch duties. In the West Country, for example, M-sets were working the main routes between Taunton, Exeter and Plymouth, together with branch services to Falmouth and Kingswear. The WW-sets seem to have

been the mainstay of the Minehead branch services at the time and also worked from Taunton to Yeovil.

From the 1930 listing, the A- and D-sets are typical of the suburban services worked by the busy urban divisions such as London and Birmingham. These would have been used primarily for fast local services along main routes, but some took in branch services as part of their daily round. Henley was one branch which regularly saw D-sets, close-coupled trains of 'Toplight' stock.

Readers should observe that these standard formations simply define the type of coaches to be used for particular workings, they do not give the style of the vehicle (i.e. the Diagram No.). For that information, it is necessary to refer to photographs where you will find that some pleasing variation re-emerges.

We will look at examples of how these sets were worked, together with the other branch trains shortly, but before that we must consider freight and non-passenger traffic.

FREIGHT STOCK

Branch passenger services were often characterised by a stability which might see the same set of coaches plying to and fro along the line for years on end. Freight

Another Didcot & Newbury line train, in the charge of a former M & SWJR 2–4–0 engine, No. 1334. The leading coach is one of the 46ft 6in vehicles built in the late 1880s to Diagram E14. In the middle of the train is one of the GWR's 'Siphons' for the carriage of milk, whilst at the tail there are two short-wheelbase coaches and another Siphon.

J. E. KITE

workings, in contrast, at least had the potential for greater variation, since the wagons, unlike many branch passenger trains, were worked off the branch into the main system. This would have brought not just a medley of Great Western wagons onto the branch, but also examples of 'foreign' companies' stock.

Freight workings, unlike passenger services, seem not to have been subject to the same detailed documentation. They ran, of course, to a timetable but, since the composition of individual freight trains was tailored more directly to meet day-to-day traffic needs, their composition could seldom be set down.

However, occasionally, written records of varying character come to light. One such example was discovered by John Copsey at the PRO at Kew, a 1925 survey of branch lines conducted by the company. Although providing only a 'snapshot' of operations at a particular time, the data do throw interesting light on the scale and character of branch freight working.

Table 6 summarises the principal details for forty of the company's branches. Direct comparison of lines isn't entirely possible as there are some inconsistencies in recording information, but I think the table is still revealing. Four categories of traffic are noted; milk, livestock, coals and minerals, and general merchandise. The main elements in the latter two categories are identified in the final column.

As an overall comment, it is clear that the majority of the lines were net importers of freight, i.e. wagons received normally outnumbered wagons forwarded. (The balance is made up of empties which are not recorded.) Movement of goods to the branch was particularly prominent in the case of coals and minerals and only four lines on the list sent more than they received in this category (Launceston, Moretonhampstead and the Tanat and Teign Valley lines). I would be fairly confident that this traffic would have been stone. Coal would always have been an import on the branches listed, except for occasional instances where a local factor might have sent the odd full wagon to another merchant or depot. To show this traffic correctly in model form, therefore, we should have loaded mineral wagons entering the branch and empties leaving, although given the constraints of operating a model railway, how we achieve this I'm not sure!

In the movement of general merchandise, the table shows that empty wagons would have to have come onto some of the branches for loading and forwarding. However, since most lines show more of a balance in inward and outward movement of general goods, that effect is easier to recreate since empty general vehicles would have been a normal sight in trains moving up and down the line.

The substantial variations in movement of milk and livestock reflects local conditions. In counties such as Wiltshire and Somerset where there was a prominent

Table 6. Freight Working on Branches – 1925

Line	Coals & Minerals Fwd	Coals & Minerals Rec	General Goods Fwd	General Goods Rec	Number of cans of milk/ annum	No. of trucks livestock/ annum	Principal Traffic
Abbotsbury	–	12	3	4	24,707	34	Coal, roadstone, flour, general goods.
Aberayron	–	6	5	8	1,031	376	Coal, roadstone, bricks, grain.
Abingdon	–	11	8	14	2,900	357	Coal, grain, farm products.
Alcester	–	5	4	7	21	89	Coal, roadstone, round timber.
Ashburton	–	12	18	20	3,111	233	Coal, timber, grain, manure.
Blenheim	–	3	2	3	2,336	96	Coal, bricks, farm products/machinery.
Bridport	4	14	19	23	61,661	569	Coal, gravel, sand, general goods.
Brixham	–	6	1	13	–	–	Coal, general goods.
Calne	–	8	44	26	98,139	4,519	Meat, bacon, pigs, general goods.
Cardigan	2	22	19	35	35,689	1,062	Coal, slates, timber, farm products.
Chard	1	2	12	23	83,789	626	Coal, general goods.
Cirencester	–	12	14	23	12,780	1,027	Grain, hay, coal, general goods.
Clevedon	–	4	3	7	2,000	53	Coal, general goods.
Falmouth	–	10	20	34	646	14,433	Granite, lime, meat.
Faringdon	–	8	7	7	56,152	370	Coal, roadstone, hay boards, tin boxes.
Hemyock	–	1	7	11	2,865	1,185	Meat, farm products.
Highworth	1	9	6	12	107,127	178	Coal, roadstone, feed, general goods.
Lambourn	–	7	21	4	21,305	68	Coal, roadstone, round timber, grain.
Launceston	30	25	20	49	13,234	946	Coal, roadstone, bricks, china clay.
Llanfyllin	–	4	6	9	1,587	926	Coal, grain, round timber.
Looe	–	4	3	4	3,512	176	Grain, manure.
Malmesbury	–	5	3	7	68,040	139	Bacon, grain, hay, coal, feed, general.
Minehead	1	18	31	37	7,165	1,064	–
M'hampstead	22	11	15	8	1,699	423	Coal, china clay, earthenware.
Newcastle Emlyn	–	24	26	24	1,239	1,620	Roadstone, pit wood, farm products.
New Radnor	4	5	17	18	1,576	1,261	Coal, roadstone, timber, farm goods.
Pembroke	16	44	30	49	32,602	1,225	Coal, roadstone, timber, farm goods.
Pontrilas	–	7	4	7	640	262	Coal, timber, grain, farm goods.
Presteign	–	2	4	3	–	–	Timber, grain, livestock.
Princetown	–	4	2	5	–	44	Coal, general goods.
St. Ives	–	9	2	9	–	93	Coal, broccoli.
Shipston	–	5	5	8	2,793	251	Coal, general goods.
Tanat Val.	36	9	4	4	903	770	Coal, roadstone, lime, limestone.
Teign Val.	40	16	5	20	807	135	Stone.
Tetbury	–	3	2	6	43,645	292	Coal, general goods.
Wadebridge	–	4	4	8	3,190	277	Roadstone.
Wallingford	–	11	20	14	7,825	258	Coal, cement, grain.
Watlington	6	17	15	8	29,087	150	Lime, cement, farm products.
Wrington V.	–	4	2	6	12,841	44	Coal, general goods.
Yealmpton	5	8	7	3	3,352	103	Coal, slate, bricks, roadstone, lime.

A lovely official view of a country station with a 'Dean Goods' engine shunting cattle trucks at Llanwrda on the Central Wales line. The train is probably a special farm removal since there are other official photos of a Dean Goods on such a train at this location.

THE WELSH INDUSTRIAL AND MARITIME MUSEUM

A general view of the yard at Lambourn revealing a typical mix of goods vehicles for a branch station. Modellers should note the preponderance of open wagons and the incidence of 'foreign' vehicles, including here the private owner coal wagon from Cannock, Staffordshire.   C. L. MOWAT

dairy industry, large volumes of milk were being moved and would have been a conspicuous aspect of traffic. Elsewhere it dwindled to negligible proportions. The survey does not provide a breakdown between cans forwarded and received but it is logical to presume that the large quantities were associated with extensive export rather than import of milk.

A similar conclusion might be true for movements of livestock, although young cattle could be imported into an area for export once fattened. However, there were still substantial contrasts with, at one extreme, Falmouth, with its important trade in meat and livestock, and at the other, Abbotsbury or Princetown, where livestock movements averaged less than one truck per week.

The listing of the principal items of freight reinforces the point made at the start of the chapter that branch lines seldom saw much specialist traffic. Coals, roadstones, timber, grain and other farm produce/equipment, and unspecified

general goods were typical of the majority. There were exceptions – Calne, for example, was famous for its bacon and sausage trade and, according to these figures, was a busy little station. The Cornish branches of St. Ives and Helston (not listed) had seasonal trade in broccoli and other vegetables. Brixham forwarded large quantities of fish but this movement was recorded as 'passenger' rather than 'goods' traffic as fish trucks were vacuum-fitted and could be worked as tail traffic on passenger trains. The same applied to the working of horse-boxes on the Lambourn branch.

What types of vehicle would have been used to carry the types of traffic listed? Coal and some of the roadstone, sand and gravel would have been carried in the fleets of private owners wagons. I would love to know more about how these were worked. There must have been complex and elaborate networks of movements between collieries, factors and merchants but if this trade was logged in detail,

records do not seem to have survived in an organised fashion. I imagine that many local merchants collected coal from large depots in the area, the depots in turn being supplied by the collieries. But from photographic evidence it seems that many firms, large and small, sent their wagons all the way to the coalfields. The safest approach for the branch modeller is probably to assume nothing and model wagons that can be identified in photos of your line or those which belonged to merchants based in the area where your model is located in cases where you are inventing a scene.

The carriage of general merchandise relied upon open wagons and covered vans (Minks) in the company ownership. Study any photograph of a goods yard on the Great Western and, discounting the private owners wagons, I guarantee that the majority of wagons will be Minks and opens. There were a very large number of different designs, particularly amongst the open wagons, including variations with vacuum brakes and with or without sheet rails for tarpaulins. As a general rule, if the merchandise was in boxes, sacks or barrels, it would travel in a Mink or open, sheeted if necessary, to keep out the rain. Timber, stone, hay and manure also went into open wagons and, although there were special wagons for the carriage of the latter two, branch lines would probably have used standard opens instead.

Carriage of milk was, for much of the Great Western's history, based upon the wooden-slatted, six-wheeled 'Siphons'. These were 'brown' vehicles, vacuum-fitted for running fast in milk trains or attached to passenger trains. Milk was originally carried in 17 gallon, conical churns, the shorter cylinders came later. These vehicles were quite appropriate for lines with 'normal' levels of milk traffic, perhaps a Siphon being attached to one of the branch trains on a daily basis. On branches where there was a specialist trade in milk, larger vehicles could be used. These included the 50 ft Siphons G and H or alternatively a passenger brake van. Some of Abbotsbury's milk was moved regularly in an elderly 40 ft PBV.

Later, milk was switched to tanks and the Siphons were displaced from their intended roles. They still continued in service, though, the open slatted Siphons often being used to move fruit and veg-etables, the enclosed Siphons G and H and the shorter Siphon F transferring to parcels traffic, though rarely in this capacity on branches, where parcels traffic seldom commanded the allocation of parcels stock. Some of the Siphon C and Siphon F vehicles were used for many years on the Calne branch transporting sausages and bacon.

Livestock was transported in the com-pany's cattle wagons and horse-boxes. Horse-boxes tended to be kept for more valuable beasts, and rural horse fairs usually saw animals arrive and depart in cattle wagons. So you don't necessarily have to have horse-boxes to move horses! Like the milk vans, cattle wagons could also be pressed into service carrying veg-etables. Broccoli trains on the Helston branch were typically comprised of cattle trucks.

The only other general service vehicle we need for our typical branch freight train is the brake van. Most branches were allocated their own brake van, the stan-dard 20-ton design being the most wide-spread. This would have been branded with the name of the station where it was usually based, commonly the branch ter-minus.

The foregoing discussion implies that the wagons used would be Great Western ones. However, this is not necessarily the case since Common User arrangements

Milk traffic was not always present on branch lines, but, as this busy 1920s scene at Stratton illustrates, traffic could be considerable.
CTY. A. T. DAGLISH/SWINDON SOCIETY

S. H. P. HIGGINS

An idyllic picture of the rural goods train with an ex-MSWJR 2—4—0 drifting down the Lambourn branch with the daily goods.

would have brought large numbers of 'foreign' wagons onto Great Western lines. Within the Common User system, LMS and LNER wagons were in a massive majority, something like 80% coming from these two companies. In contrast the GWR contributed just 15% and the SR only 5%. Special wagons which were not subject to Common User arrangements were clearly branded as such. But this does mean that for our typical branch scene for the 1920s and '30s, we should include a suitable balance in which Great Western wagons would be considerably outnumbered by 'foreign' wagons.

WORKING THE LINE

So far we have seen something of the types of vehicles and formations that constituted the mainstay of branch line services. The question remains, however, as to how the trains were worked.

A local goods train entering Milverton on the Barnstaple line behind an unidentified Dean Goods engine.
LENS OF SUTTON

Dean Goods No. 2573 working another Lambourn line freight train.

J. F. RUSSELL-SMITH

If we return again to the 1925 survey of branches, information recorded therein provides illustration of the frequency of services on the respective lines and the degree to which passenger and freight movements were merged or separated. *Table 7* summarises the information.

The full range of branch traffic conditions is illustrated, from the busy lines such as the Falmouth and Launceston branches at one extreme to the truly sleepy branches to Presteign or Shipston at the other. The majority of lines, though, typically saw between six and eight trains a day, with one or sometimes two goods services. This perhaps acts as a rough guide to the level of service we might incorporate in a model if we are chasing that elusive, authentic flavour. There were some interesting exceptions to common patterns. Calne, for example, was sufficiently important to warrant three goods trains a day, whilst several routes reveal attractive combinations of branch passenger sets, auto trains, mixed trains and pure freight services. So there are alternatives if the commonplace does not appeal.

The notes on passenger workings hint at the complexity of patterns which could be encountered on some branches and these invite some further illustration. There were, in fact, several ways in which passenger services on branch lines could be organised. The simplest pattern was where a branch train, be it a rake of coaches, an auto-trailer or a railmotor, effectively 'lived' on the line and shuttled to and fro between the terminus and the junction. I think it is true to say that the majority were of this type and there would be no variation in the allocation of passenger stock and the manner in which it worked for months, often years, at a time. Some services of this type were incredibly intensive and really were shuttle services in the true sense of the word. For example, the railmotor working the short branch from Stourbridge Town to Stourbridge Junction during 1914 made almost 60 trips each way, daily, Monday to Saturday!

However, more complex patterns were possible in which rather than a set of coaches or a vehicle working back and forwards between two places, it would cover a network of routes. An example is given in *Table 8* which shows the routeing for a Kidderminster-based railmotor working in the Severn Valley in 1911. In running this pattern, this railmotor is 'dovetailing' with other workings which together provided the full service for the places listed.

Table 7. Summary of Services on Branches – 1925

Line	Passenger Traffic *worked by*	Goods Traffic *worked by*
Abbotsbury	Railmotor 5 trips e/w.	Goods Train, MO, WO, SO.
Aberayron	Auto Train 4 trips e/w.	Goods Train, 1 e/w daily.
Abingdon	⌈14 trips + 3 mixed (up) ⌊15 trips + 2 mixed (dn).	Goods Train, 2 e/w daily plus mixed trips.
Alcester	Autocar 6 trips e/w.	Mixed trips, 2 e/w daily.
Ashburton	Branch Train 7 trips e/w.	Goods Train, 1 e/w daily.
Blenheim	⌈8 trips + 1 mixed (dn) ⌊6 trips + 3 mixed (up).	Goods Train, 1 e/w daily plus mixed trips.
Bridport	6 trips + 1 mixed e/w.	Goods Train, 2 up, 1 dn plus mixed trips.
Brixham	15 trips + 1 mixed e/w.	Goods Train, 1 e/w daily plus mixed trips.
Calne	Auto/R'motor 8 trips e/w.	Goods Trains, 3 e/w daily.
Cardigan	Branch Train 1 trip plus 3 mixed e/w.	Goods Trains, 2 e/w daily plus mixed trips.
Chard	6 trips e/w + 1 SO.	Goods trains, 2 e/w daily.
Cirencester	⌈8 trips + 3 mixed (dn) ⌊6 trips + 4 mixed (up).	Goods Train, 1 e/w daily plus mixed trips.
Clevedon	⌈Branch Train 3 trips e/w ⌊Railmotor 18 trips e/w.	Goods Train, 1 e/w daily.
Falmouth	14 trips + 1 mixed e/w.	Goods Train, 2 e/w daily plus mixed trips.
Faringdon	11 trips e/w including 9 mixed; 4dn, 5 up.	Mixed Trains only.
Hemyock	5 trips e/w inc 4 mixed.	Mixed Trains only.
Highworth	6 trips e/w inc 1 mixed.	Goods Train, 1 e/w daily plus mixed trips.
Lambourn	Branch Train 5 trips e/w.	Goods Train, 1 e/w daily.
Launceston	15 trips e/w; 11 to T'stock, 4 to Launceston.	Goods Trains, 3 e/w daily 1 only to Launceston.
Llanfyllin	Branch Train 5 trips e/w.	Goods Train, 1 e/w daily.
Looe	7 trips + 1 mixed (dn) 8 trips (up).	Goods Train, 1 e/w daily plus mixed trips.
Malmesbury	7 trips e/w including 5 mixed; 3 (dn) and 2 (up).	Mixed Trains only.
Minehead	7 trips e/w.	Goods Trains, 2 e/w daily 1 to Washford only.
M'hampstead	Branch Train 10 trips + Railmotor 1 trip e/w	Goods Trains, 3 e/w daily 2 to Heathfield only.
Newcastle Emlyn	7 trips e/w, 6 SO.	Goods Trains, 2 e/w daily additional RR.
New Radnor	3 trips e/w	Goods Train, 1 e/w daily.
Pembroke	⌈Branch Train 5 trips (dn) ⌊4 trips (up) Auto car 2 trips e/w.	Goods Trains, 2 e/w daily.
Pontrilas	3 mixed trips e/w.	Mixed Trains only.
Presteign	3 trips e/w.	Goods Trains, 2 RR e/w one once a week, other once a fortnight.
Princetown	5 trips e/w.	Goods Train, 1 e/w e.o.d.
St. Ives	15 trips e/w.	Goods Train, 1 e/w daily.
Shipston	3 mixed trips e/w.	Mixed Trains only.
Teign Valley	Auto Train 6 trips e/w.	Goods Trains, 3 e/w daily.
Tetbury	Branch Train 6 trips e/w including 2 mixed.	Goods Trains, 1 e/w daily plus mixed trips.
Wadebridge	10 trips e/w.	Goods Trains, 3 e/w daily 7 (RR) trips.
Wallingford	14 trips e/w inc 3 mixed.	Goods Train, 1 dn only plus mixed trips.
Watlington	6 trips e/w.	Goods Trains, 2 e/w daily.
Wrington Vale	Branch Train 3 trips e/w Railmotor 1 trip e/w.	Goods Train, 1 e/w daily.
Yealmpton	Auto Train 9 trips e/w.	Goods Train, 1 e/w daily.

Abbreviations: MO   Monday Only
                 WO   Wednesday Only
                 SO   Saturday Only
                 e/w   each way
                 RR   runs as required
                 e.o.d.   every other day

Table 8. Daily Working of Kidderminster Railmotor No. 1 – July 1911

am	
5.42	Kidderminster – Stourbridge Junct.
6.20	Stourbridge Junct. – Stourbridge
6.26	Stourbridge – Stourbridge Junct.
6.33	Stourbridge Junct. – Kidderminster
7.05	Kidderminster – Stourport
7.30	Stourport – Bewdley
7.46	Bewdley – Hartlebury
8.40	Hartlebury – Kidderminster
then	Kidderminster – Hartlebury and Return until
pm	
1.23	Kidderminster – Bewdley
2.20	Bewdley – Hartlebury
4.05	Hartlebury – Kidderminster and Return
5.20	Hartlebury – Bewdley
5.45	Bewdley – Stourport and Return
6.14	Bewdley – Kidderminster
6.45	Kidderminster – Hartlebury
7.17	Hartlebury – Bridgnorth
9.25	Bridgnorth – Kidderminster

Stourbridge Town station with a steam railmotor on the short shuttle service to Stourbridge Junction. At the height of the service, as many as sixty trips were run each way between the two stations.

Bewdley, with one of the Kidderminster-based railmotors standing at Platform 1. This is a 70ft vehicle built in 1908 to Diagram R, one of the last to be built for the GWR. The rear of the railmotor is obscured by a through coach from the LNWR. The roof board gives the destination as Birmingham. It would have been detached from an LNWR train at Woofferton Junction on the Shrewsbury–Hereford line and would have reached Bewdley via Tenbury Wells.

A fascinating scene at St. Ives, shortly before the outbreak of the Second World War. Prairie tank No. 4517 has just arrived with a local train conveying the through coach off the 'Cornish Riviera Ltd'. Through coaches were usually brake composites and this is one of the 'Centenary' vehicles introduced in 1935. Note the small destination board for 'St. Ives' beneath the main roof board. In the foreground are some interesting road vehicles including a hotel bus sent to meet incoming guests, whilst in the background the beach is crowded with holidaymakers, most of whom would have come by train.

COLLECTION P. KARAU

Or to provide a more complex and fuller example, we may consider the working of the line from Plymouth to Tavistock and Launceston at the same period. Here there was no permanent branch set as such, the service being provided by local sets working a range of services in the Plymouth Division. For the weekday service, no less than five sets contributed to working the branch. The basic service was provided by Sets Nos. 52 and 54 (*Table 9*).

There are two points to note. First, working No. 54 was confined to the branch whereas No. 52 provided part of the late afternoon service to Plympton and back. Secondly, each was a 'daily' working in which the coaches ended up back at their starting point, ready to repeat the service the following day.

These trains all served Tavistock on their way to and from Launceston, but the traffic on the Tavistock–Plymouth section was sufficiently extensive to warrant additional services for that part of the branch. These were provided by three further sets, Nos. 18, 22 and 27. Set 27 provided an early evening return service only, and is not illustrated (*Table 10*).

Set No. 22 I think warrants no further comment since its pattern is very like Nos. 52 and 54, but No. 18 is more interesting since it doesn't return to its starting point. In fact, it would take a rake of coaches working as Set No. 18 two further days to find its way back to form the 7.10 am from Exeter. In the process it would work the next day as Set 19, serving Plymouth, Exeter, Newton Abbot and Saltash and then the following day as Set 20, serving Liskeard, Plymouth, Newton Abbot and ending up at Kingswear. The Working Programme does not state it, but I presume the coaches then worked overnight as empty coaching stock (ECS) to Exeter, to begin the cycle again. Therefore, to provide local working No. 18 on the Tavistock section of the branch on a daily basis, three rakes of coaches would be required.

I have tried to illustrate the complexity of coach working primarily to remind modellers not to make assumptions concerning the allocations of vehicles to services. In a sense, a branch timetable can be misleading because it simply states when a service ran but gives no indication of how many different trains were involved. But from the Launceston branch example we can see, for instance, that the 9.43 am

service from Tavistock to Plymouth was quite different in composition from the 5.27 pm service and that to model the daily service accurately, we would actually need five rakes of coaches. The branch modeller need not, therefore, be necessarily constrained to modest and limited programmes of stock construction if he chooses a line where these more complex patterns of operations were used.

These branch sets and other local workings were augmented in some instances by the working of through coaches onto branch lines. To illustrate the extent and character of these services I have again selected a single programme as an example, this time for July 1921. All of the through workings to branches at that date are listed in *Table 11*.

I think the point which strikes one most forcibly is just how limited these workings were. Other listings I have made, for example for 1927, are longer but not dramatically so. With the exception of Fairford and Calne, all of the destinations listed were quite significant places on the passenger network.

Secondly, it is important to note the type of vehicle typically used for through workings. With the exception of Henley which received a set of four coaches off the 5.15 pm from Paddington to Weston-super-Mare, the majority of the remainder were served by a single Brake Composite, usually a 70 ft vehicle. Slip coach workings to serve branches were rare and where they did occur, they tended to be reserved for the larger stations. In the 1921 list,

Table 9. Plymouth Division Sets 52 and 54 – Launceston Branch 1911

No. 52	(*Van, 2 Compos, 2 Thirds, Van Third*).	No. 54	(*Van, 2 Compos, 2 Thirds, Van Third*).
7.30 am	Launceston – Plymouth	7.20 am	Plymouth – Launceston
11.05 am	Plymouth – Launceston	9.55 am	Launceston – Plymouth
1.50 pm	Launceston – Plymouth	2.45 pm	Plymouth – Launceston
4.33 pm	Plymouth – Plympton	6.22 pm	Launceston – Plymouth
5.05 pm	Plympton – Plymouth		
7.10 pm	Plymouth – Launceston	(Changes one day a week with Set 22 for cleaning purposes).	

Table 10. Plymouth Division Sets 18 and 22 – Launceston Branch 1911

No. 18	(*B-set, 6-wheeled stock*)	No. 22	(*Van, 2 Compos, 2 Thirds, Van Third*)
7.10 am	Exeter – Plymouth	6.28 am	Plymouth – Tavistock
10.06 am	Plymouth – Tavistock	7.22 am	Tavistock – Plymouth
11.30 am	Tavistock – Plymouth	8.47 am	Plymouth – Tavistock
1.57 pm	Plymouth – Tavistock	9.43 am	Tavistock – Plymouth
5.27 pm	Tavistock – Plymouth	11.50 am	Plymouth – Saltash SO
7.25 pm	Plymouth – Liskeard	1.03 pm	Saltash – Plymouth SO
8.30 pm	Liskeard – Plymouth	5.08 pm	Plymouth – Tavistock
10.05 pm	Plymouth – Liskeard	9.46 pm	Tavistock – Plymouth
		(Changes one day a week with Set 54 for cleaning purposes).	

Table 11. Through Workings to Branches – July 1921

Destination	Vehicle	Worked off	Returned by
Calne	Van	7.30 Padd–Taunton	19.05 ex Calne
St. Ives	70'Bk Compo	10.30 Padd–Penzance	9.40 ex St. Ives
Falmouth	70'Bk Compo	10.30 Padd–Penzance	10.10 ex Falmouth
Minehead	70'Bk Compo	10.30 Padd–Penzance	11.20 ex Minehead
Kingsbridge	70'Bk Compo	11.00 Padd–Plymouth	10.55 ex Kingsbridge
Newquay	70'Bk Compo	12.00 Padd–Kingswear	11.55 ex Newquay
Henley	⎧Bk Compo⎫ Third First ⎩Bk Compo⎭	}17.15 Paddington– Weston-super-Mare	}10.00 ex Henley
Aberystwyth	70'Bk Compo	11.50 Padd–Neyland	9.40 ex Aberystwyth
Pembroke Dock	60'Bk Compo	8.45 Padd–Fishguard	10.15 ex Pembroke Dock
Pembroke Dock	⎧70'Bk Compo⎫ ⎩60'Van 3rd ⎭	}11.50 Padd–Neyland	}10.15 ex Pembroke Dock
Pembroke Dock	Van	21.25 Padd–Neyland	14.00 ex Pembroke Dock
Fairford	⎧Milk Truck ⎫ ⎩Siphon × 2⎭	}14.28 ex Padd	}6.30 ex Worcester
Calne	Siphon C	11.55 Crewe–Bristol	20.00 ex Bristol
Henley	Slip	21.15 Padd–Neyland	11.10 ex Henley (SX) 10.00 ex Henley (SO)

only Henley amongst the branch stations received a slip, a late evening service off the 9.15 pm Paddington to Neyland.

Thirdly, through working of van traffic was also sporadic. I am aware that in the course of this chapter, I have hardly touched upon passenger brake vans and other service vehicles. However, with few exceptions, they were not a conspicuous feature of branch operations and there were very few through workings of vans to branches in any of the coach programmes I have studied. In the 1921 programme, only Fairford (with its milk traffic) and Calne (with its trade in sausages and bacon) had regular workings of passenger-rated vans.

Small quantities of milk were normally worked in six-wheeled Siphons attached to one of the regular branch trains, or even in the guard's compartments of Van Thirds etc. According to the 1921 working timetable for the Faringdon branch, a Siphon was detached from the 5.33 am

Paddington to Swindon and forwarded by the 8.45 am Uffington to Faringdon service. It returned the same day via the 6.15 pm from Faringdon, attached initially to the 6.20 pm Swindon to Reading local passenger.

One of the large nine-tank gas wagons. These would have served larger destinations. For lesser stations a small gas wagon was often used with two longitudinal tanks, in contrast to the transverse tanks used here.
                                                                                              J. H. RUSSELL

The only other special vehicles which would have been seen as a regular working to branches were the gas wagons used to replenish coaches with gas lighting. These were worked from the company's oil gas works at places such as Swindon, Worc-

By the middle of the 1930s milk tanks had largely replaced carriage in churns, at least for bulk deliveries. This BR-period photograph shows 0–6–0 pannier tank No. 7407 on a short milk train on the Aberayron branch in West Wales. The importance of the creamery at Felin Fach meant these trains continued to operate after passenger services were withdrawn.
                                                                                              W. A. CAMWELL

Faringdon, c.1947, with a typical mixed train of the period entering the station. Having run around its train, the engine would detach the goods vehicles and propel them into the yard which lay to the left of this view. If there were wagons to be taken with the next departure, the coach would also have to be shunted to enable the goods vehicles to be marshalled at the rear of the train.   J. H. RUSSELL

ester and Wolverhampton, normally as tail traffic on local passenger trains. For this reason their movements were listed in coach working programmes for the local divisions.

Finally, let us return briefly to the freight scene. *Table 6* has provided a flavour of how freight was moved, the two main options being a regular working of one or two goods trains per day or the alternative movement of wagons as tail traffic in mixed trains with coaches. Instructions in the General Appendix to the Rule Book stipulated that goods vehicles would *always* be placed to the rear of the passenger vehicles.

Because goods traffic workings were not documented in the same manner as passenger trains, there is much less that can be said with authority as to precisely how wagons were worked. However, there were exceptions, and one freight movement that was documented in detail was the working of station trucks. These ran daily along specified routes, calling at pre-determined stations to set down or pick up freight. There were several hundred station trucks working the system at any one time and most branches were served by their own truck. In the normal course

of events they were covered vans (Minks) and would be vacuum-fitted.

The function of the station truck was to provide a basic, regular service between major shipment centres (Paddington, Bristol, Cardiff etc) and areas of the system or particular branch lines. They also provided a facility for moving small loads between stations along the routes on which they worked. Paper labels listing stations to be served were attached to the van, and these provided space to show for which of the stations on the route the truck contained goods. Packages might be added to the truck as it progressed and an interesting article in the *Great Western Magazine* for 1935 shows examples of how labels were amended to reflect the changing contents of the truck. Each truck was internally organised so that packages for the various stations had their own area of floor space. This was arranged so that the early calling points were allocated space adjacent to the doors whilst goods for the last stations were stowed in the corners. The floor layout was shown on the van label so that, at a glance, staff at a station could see whether the truck contained anything for them and if so, where within the van it was located.

The station truck for Faringdon came from Paddington off the 12.55 am to Gloucester (4.55 am at Uffington) and would have been worked down the branch by the first train of the day. After it had been unloaded and then loaded with goods to go in the opposite direction, it was worked back to Paddington the same evening.

When freight wagons were set down at a station they would be subject to some form of shunting. There is a temptation on model layouts to overdo the shunting of the yard. (I know it's fun for operators and keeps the crowds at exhibitions interested.) However, on the real railway, a lot of branch station shunting was far more perfunctory than we like to think. For a start, staff at most stations used pinch bars and some even kept or borrowed a horse for moving wagons along a siding (a tricky one for modellers!), and the branch engine might only make one or two sorties a day into the yard. This was almost standard procedure at many small through stations where a string of wagons would simply be pushed into the yard and left at the nearest convenient location. Engines rarely followed wagons right into sidings – but left them to roll along with their own momentum to be braked by the shunter. The pin-point locating of each wagon into its alloted spot or the teasing out of individual trucks from awkward locations – the sort of movements in which we all like to indulge in running our models – were not a typical part of working a yard.

I hope my readers won't feel I'm trying to take the fun out of running a model railway by pointing out these little 'inconsistencies' in our view of the real thing. I have no intention of necessarily running my own model of Faringdon 'according to the book'. I, and any viewing public, would be comatose in no time. However, I *do* think it important that we at least recognise liberties when we choose to take them. As I have tried to show in this chapter, the Great Western branch was run according to a carefully laid out set of procedures and practices, which dictated how lines were worked and what types

of stock were appropriate for branch line duties. And if we want to produce the authentic model railway – a railway which truly represents the Great Western in miniature – then the closer we can get to these working practices, the more convincing that result should be.

In Part 3 of this study, we will consider how both the technical aspects and the atmosphere of the prototype, which we have explored in some detail in the first two books, can be captured in miniature.

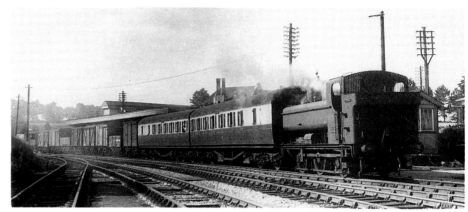

An impressive mixed train leaving Kemble for Cirencester behind 0–6–0 pannier tank No. 8779 on 6th September 1952. The passenger vehicles are a B-set.   H. C. CASSERLEY

Perhaps a more characteristic mixed train? An unidentified 2–4–0 'large Metro' tank swinging off the Brixham branch and into Churston station, propelling its auto trailer and pulling just a single van.
HMRS

BIBLIOGRAPHY

I list below the sources which I used in preparing this volume. Readers requiring further elaboration of specific themes might wish to consult the books and articles identified.

Barrie, D. S. *The Taff Vale Railway*, Oakwood Press 1939.

Barrie, D. S. *The Rhymney Railway*, Oakwood Press 1952.

Bartholomew, D. *The Midland & South Western Junction Railway* Vol. 1, Wild Swan Publications 1982.

Beale, G. 'The Standard Buildings of William Clarke', *British Railway Journal* No. 8, 1985.

Beck, K. M. *The West Midland Lines of the GWR*, Ian Allan 1983.

Beck, K. M. *The Greatness of the Great Western*, Ian Allan 1984.

Beck, K. M. *The Great Western North of Wolverhampton*, Ian Allan 1986.

Beck, K. M. 'Kingswear for Dartmouth', *British Railway Journal* No. 15, 1987.

Beck, K. M. & Copsey, J. *The Great Western in South Devon*, Wild Swan Publications 1990.

Biddle, G. & Nock, O. S. *The Railway Heritage of Britain*, Michael Joseph 1983.

Carpenter, R. 'Symonds Yat Station', *British Railway Journal* No. 4, 1984.

Chapman, C. *The Cowbridge Railway*, OPC 1984.

Clarke, R. H. *An Historical Survey of Selected Great Western Stations* (Three volumes), OPC 1976, 1979, 1981.

Harrison, I. *Great Western Railway Locomotive Allocations for 1921*, Wild Swan Publications.

HMRS *Great Western Way*, Historical Model Railway Society 1978.

Holden, J. S. *The Manchester & Milford Railway*, Oakwood Press 1979.

Jackson, B. L. *The Abbotsbury Branch*, Wild Swan Publications 1989.

Jackson, B. L. & Tattershall, M. J. *The Bridport Branch*, OPC 1976.

Jenkins, S. C. *The Fairford Branch*, Oakwood Press, 1985.

Jenkins, S. C. *The Woodstock Branch*, Wild Swan Publications 1987.

Jenkins, S. C. 'The Falmouth Branch', *British Railway Journal* No. 27, 1989.

Jenkins, S. C. 'The Shipston-on-Stour Branch – a little known outpost of the GWR', *British Railway Journal* No. 12, 1986.

Jenkins, S. C. & Pomroy, L. J. *The Moretonhampstead & South Devon Railway*, Oakwood Press 1989.

Karau, P. *Great Western Branch Line Termini* Vol. 1, OPC 1977. (Describes Fairford, Lambourn, Tetbury, Wallingford and Watlington.)

Karau, P. *Great Western Branch Line Termini* Vol. 2, OPC 1978. (Describes Abbotsbury, Ashburton, Hemyock, Moretonhampstead and Princetown.)

Karau, P. *The Henley-on-Thames Branch,* Wild Swan Publications 1982.

Karau, P. 'Common Light Railway Architecture', *British Railway Journal* Nos. 1 and 3, 1983/4.

Karau, P. 'Lost Termini – Chipping Norton', *British Railway Journal* No. 6, 1985.

Karau, P. & Turner, C. *The Wallingford Branch*, Wild Swan Publications 1982.

Karau, P. & Turner, C. *The Marlow Branch*, Wild Swan Publications (undated).

Karau, P., Parsons, M. & Robertson, K. *The Didcot, Newbury & Southampton Railway*, Wild Swan Publications 1981.

Krause, I. *Great Western Branch Line Album*, Ian Allan 1969.

Kingdom, A. R. *The Yealmpton Branch*, OPC 1974.

Kingdom, A. R. *The Princetown Branch*, OPC 1979.

Lambert, A. J. *West Midland Branch Line Album*, Ian Allan 1978.

Leigh, C. *GWR Country Stations*, Ian Allan 1981.

Leigh, C. *GWR Country Stations* Vol. 2, Ian Allan 1984.

Lingard, R. *The Princes Risborough – Thame – Oxford Railway*, OPC 1978.

Lloyd, M. *The Tanat Valley Light Railway*, Wild Swan Publications 1990.

Logan, R. 'Culham Goods Shed', *Model Railway Journal* No. 21.

Maggs, C. G. *The Clevedon Branch*, Wild Swan Publications 1987.

Maggs, C. G. *The Calne Branch*, Wild Swan Publications 1990.

Maggs, C. G. & Beale, G. *The Camerton Branch*, Wild Swan Publications 1985.

Owen, J. *The Exe Valley Railway*, Kingfisher Publications 1985.

Pocock, N. & Harrison, I. *Great Western Railway Locomotive Allocations for 1934*, Wild Swan Publications.

Pope, I., How, R. & Karau, P. *The Severn & Wye Railway* (Three volumes), Wild Swan Publications 1983, 1985, 1988.

Potts, C. R. *The Brixham Branch*, Oakwood Press 1986.

Potts, C. R. *An Historical Survey of Selected Great Western Stations* Vol. 4, OPC 1985.

Randolph, S. *The Tetbury Branch*, Wild Swan Publications 1985.

Robertson, K. & Simmonds, R. *The Lambourn Branch*, Wild Swan Publications 1984.

Russell, J. H. *The Banbury & Cheltenham Railway*, OPC 1984.

Signalling Study Group *The Signal Box*, OPC 1987.

Smith, T. M. & Heathcliffe, G. S. *The Highworth Branch*, Wild Swan Publications 1979.

Trippett, N. & de Courtais, N. *The Abingdon Branch*, Wild Swan Publications 1985.

Vaughan, A. *A History of the Faringdon Branch & Uffington Station*, OPC 1979.

Vaughan, A. *A Pictorial Record of Great Western Architecture*, OPC 1977.

Whitehouse, P. & St. John Thomas, D. *The Great Western Railway*, David & Charles 1984.

INDEX

Page Numbers may indicate the start of a section and refer to either pictures or text.